P9-ARU-831

The Pseudo-Ethic

A SPECULATION ON AMERICAN
POLITICS AND MORALS

by

Margaret Halsey

SIMON AND SCHUSTER · NEW YORK · 1963

First Printing

Library of Congress Catalog Card Number: 63–17724
Manufactured in the United States of America
By The Book Press, Brattleboro, Vermont

CONTENTS

———•—•———

65080

CONTENTS

The Pseudo-Ethic

I

A Preface to Be Read

THIS BOOK has been given the subtitle of "a speculation" in response to the fact that present-day Americans are strongly conditioned to respect science and statistics. Many of them, indeed, think of science (inaccurately) as an area of unfailing mathematical exactitude where imagination has no place at all. When, therefore, writers deal with problems in the area of the social sciences, they are apt to get scant attention unless they come confidently forward, Carmen-like, wearing the Gross National Product like a rose over one ear.

The G.N.P. or some other real, visible, tangible fact.

But the adjuration to "Be realistic" merely means "Agree with me, and think the way I think." No one ever says, either to himself or out loud, "My thinking is unrealistic." There is, however, more than one way to be realistic. Facts are fine, but they can obscure reality, and our American concern with "getting the facts" sometimes seems to do just that. The idea around which this book is written was arrived at by intuition; but intuition, just as much as "scientific research," can be based on accurately observed reality. It merely omits from consciousness some of the steps between observation and conclusion.

It is the writer's hope that the interpretation of recent moral history set forth here may prove to be a shared intuition and that many readers will feel that they, too, have sensed the same thing.

If intuition in the field of the social sciences needs no defense, the choice of ethics as subject for this kind of discussion may require a word of explanation. Ethics—or rather, its opposite, moral delinquency—is something that everyone knows about. The fondness of Americans for being scolded about commercialism and corruption has become almost a joke. The works of Vance Packard and books like Thomas Griffith's *The Waist-High Culture*, Russell Lynes's *A Surfeit of Honey* and August Heckscher's *The Public Happiness* are appreciatively reviewed and their disparaging texts are read with something like relish. Indeed, in this self-denigrating atmosphere it is not difficult to get a letter into the *Times* or an article into a liberal magazine describing the contemporary scene in extremely unflattering terms.

But one thing appears to be common to all these complaints.

Whatever their superficial eloquence, they have a uniform undertone of acceptance and resignation. It is permissible to complain about the spiritual blight of the consuming society, but the complaint *must* be accompanied by an intimation, explicit or implicit, that the way that society is going is inevitable and unavoidable. However vigorous the headshaking, the underlying message is always one of helplessness. "This thing is too big for the both of us."

But suppose one regarded commercialism and corruption as surface phenomena, and tried to dig deeper? Suppose one were to assert that there are other possible attitudes than resignation and acceptance? How difficult would it be to be heard?

Roger Hagan, writing in the September, 1961, issue of *Contact* on "American Response to Change," speaks of a sense of emptiness as being prevalent among present-day Americans and adds:

One characteristic of the sense of emptiness is the fear of loss of control, a fear which makes for rigidity and suspicion of new proposals and alternative courses. I think this is behind the retreat of many Americans into a sort of anti-intellectual "show-me" stance when confronted with anyone who argues that change for the better is possible and that there are some ideas available to point the way.

Indeed, American life has lately become so meretricious that for some affirmative people only one course of conduct has seemed to be open and that is to withdraw and live, so far as emotions are concerned, outside the culture. Such people eat, sleep and pay income tax within the borders of the United States, but they reject the practices and attitudes of the society around them and they stubbornly insist, not only on the necessity for change (everyone agrees on that), but on the *possibility* of change.

Of course, they are regarded as outsiders.

For the outsiders, the current rhetoric about commercialism and corruption is a mere picking at scabs. In fact, it is worse, for by talking so much about dishonesty, acquisitiveness, etcetera, the headshakers only set up the self-fulfilling prophecy and bring about an increase in the very qualities they ostensibly deplore.

The outsiders, on the other hand, see commercialization and corruption as symptoms—symptoms which can be cured by changing the human institutions which cause them. Something fresh, therefore, may still be said on the hackneyed subject of today's ethics.

And perhaps even something hopeful.

To live outside the culture is lonely. The insiders make a cult of the Kennedys and smile and salaam in companionable admiration, whereas to the outsider the Kennedys seem merely a well-dressed Massachusetts version of the Snopes family. Among the insiders, the fashionable new word is Establishment, whereas the outsider is passionately concerned with Disestablishment—i.e., with changes that would make a real difference, like discrediting, and doing away with the practice of, planned obsolescence.

Inside the culture, there is a continual, reassuring incantation—in books, newspapers, magazines, radio-television, private conversation—of Ritual Lies. The phrase is actually less harsh than it sounds, because the Ritual Lies are felt, comfortably, as ritual and not as lies. (When they begin to be felt as lies, they are abandoned. For instance, the premise of the innate inferiority of Negroes was a Ritual Lie of some time back which is now in process of being abandoned, though only after a struggle on the part of Negroes which began earlier and involved more bitterness than one could have deduced from reading the Caucasian press. A Ritual Lie of smaller dimensions, now completely abandoned, was the liturgical chant that whatever you might think of Richard Nixon, he would certainly make a strong President.)

Inside the culture, for all the reassuring like-mindedness and the cozy, voluptuous contempt for any non-liturgical utterances, there is a mood of paralyzed despair. The outsiders, on the other hand, have room for hope. They can hope because they have no particular reverence for the institutions that create commercialism and corruption. They see these institutions as man-made and thus accessible to change. Hence the outsiders, despite their loneliness, can sometimes (they think) catch glimpses of "the wintry smile upon the face of truth."

To many people the very word "ethics" sounds priggish. To others a discussion of today's ethics is a waste of time. They admit we are having a walk on the wild side right now, but all through history man's behavior has swung pendulum-like between relatively good and notably bad, hasn't it?

Undeniably.

Standards of morality were comparatively high in the early Roman Republic and again centuries later under Marcus Aurelius and the Antonines; but depravity was a household word during the reign of Caligula. In our own country and our own times, commercialism and corruption seemed so rampant during the 1920's that artists, sensitive to the climate—people like Ernest Hemingway—fled to Europe; and that same era saw Woodrow Wilson's idealism tragically done to death.

The Great Depression in the next decade purged away some of the dross, but in these affluent times the dross appears to have returned a hundredfold.

These alternations between bad and slightly better may sometimes seem superficial (corruption—reform—corruption—reform has been, for instance, a standard pattern of American politics) but they are also oftentimes revealing of deeper things. Today's ethics reflect the fact that America has become in recent years a one-institution society. Sparta was a one-institution society, the single institution being militarism.

Europe in the Middle Ages, before the rise of the nation-states, was similarly organized, the dominant institution being the Church. In such a society, the single institution tends to be so much in the ascendant that there is no place you can go to get away from it. In the United States today, the dominant institution is business.

Business is so ubiquitous that, except to those outside the culture, its ascendancy is almost not visible.

Farming is now a mechanized industry.

Education, at least on the college level, has become a threshing floor for the great corporations.

Philanthropy is keyed to tax evasion and is dominated by huge foundations set up with industrial fortunes.

Scientific research, even in universities, hardly exists except as sponsored by corporations or by a government that runs interference for business.

In politics, the electorate is treated like a body of consumers, not a body of voters, and Eisenhower's backers openly avowed their candidate would be sold "like toothpaste."

Organized religion has taken over the business techniques of promotion and public relations, and as to the family, *The New York Times* * begins a prominent news article by saying "The American teen-ager, in his increasingly important role as a consumer, is being courted as never before by the nation's retailers and manufacturers."

* May 20, 1962.

A distinguished foreign observer noted some years ago that in America, business is so important it has a special ethos of its own. "Special ethos" is a euphemism. It stands for cutting corners; and as business became the dominant, inescapable institution of our society, it was inevitable that the ethos once supposedly limited to business people during business hours should become the ethos of everything and everybody all around the clock.

The point is clear enough.

Or is it?

For a paradox begins to emerge, as we look at America becoming, with the unceasing expansion of business, a one-institution society.

Most people think our problem today is too much complexity. No single person, even a genius, can know more than the tiniest fraction of what there is to know. And yet *a one-institution society is simple, unsophisticated, almost a primitive social pattern*. Labor-saving devices, advanced medicine, the conquest of space and all the other showy phenomena of the surface seem to indicate headlong, tumultuous social progress. But underneath, our society has gone backward rather than forward.

What follows in this book is a speculation on the *how* and *why* of that regression, with particular reference to a new pseudo-ethic which, it is postulated, was the instrument that brought the regression about. Since the essay is written from the outsider's point of view, it is not devoid of hope; but "outside" and "inside" are categories which need not be regarded too inflexibly, for they can sometimes intermingle. The following sentence, for instance, sounds like an outsider's commentary, but it was written by one of the most notable insiders of all time, the Duke of Wellington:

"All the wise men were on one side, and all the damned fools were on the other, and by gad, Sir, the damned fools were right." *

One last prefatory note is necessary.

This writer believes that as a general thing, social and political essays are more dignified if they omit the personal, but because of the climate in which we have been living for the past ten or fifteen years, one small reference of that nature seems advisable.

When the idea of publishing the ensuing material was discussed, friends said warningly, "They'll call you a Communist." To this the answer must be subjoined that "they" already have. Three years ago I was approached by a well-known lecture bureau with the suggestion that I speak under its auspices, but my career as a lecturer quickly came to an end because I was too "controversial" a figure. This is not to say that where the trouble arose, it arose because I was scheduled to speak on politics, sociology or economics. I was booked to give a humorous lecture on women's fashions, shopping in supermarkets, and other distaff subjects. But the right-wingers said I was dangerous;

* Quoted by Arnold J. Toynbee in *Greek Civilization and Character*.

the clubs, sororities and sisterhoods did not want "trouble"; and nobody mentioned the issue of freedom of speech.

Once, as a matter of fact, the charge of "Communism" was raised, and on that particular occasion made, quite literally, to stick. In the early fifties, a few months before Ed Murrow did his famous program on McCarthy, I gave a speech on McCarthyism in the place where I live. As a result, somebody came in the night and painted "Dirty Communist" and a string of obscenities on the screens of my side porch. Since I live in a decorous neighborhood, these sentiments glowed, up and down our street, like a lighted cigar-end in a summer dusk.

But one of the things about being called a Communist is that, although the sense of outrage and of injustice is hard to bear, eventually you come out on the other side. My motives have been impugned, my property defaced, my voice silenced and a profitable source of income cut off; but I can speak my mind with freedom because there is nothing left to lose.

Of course, the word "Communist" has become such a basilisk collection of syllables that even the most liberated intellect is likely to have a fleeting moment of thinking that where there's smoke, there's fire and perhaps she . . .

However, despite all the *Sturm und Drang* which developed about them, the "movements" and "united fronts" of the 1930's were not so big that the participants thereof were faceless and anonymous. The seasoned veterans of the radical impulse know that whatever fights they made in that earlier time, they made without assistance from me. Other matters preoccupied me in those days, and I was late in developing an interest in social issues. Hence, I have had only that amount of brainwashing which is effected by the Episcopal Church operating on a somewhat literal-minded child—with perhaps a few pats, tweaks and finishing touches put on by the Unitarians when I grew up. It should not be necessary in a free country to write any such introduction, but writers are naturally anxious to get their points across, and it seemed possible that these pages might be read more attentively if it were understood that the author did not come in on a left wing, but on a prayer.

II

The Malady Lingers On

THERE SEEMS LITTLE NEED to demonstrate, by marshaling evidence, that a mongrelization of ethics has taken place in the United States since the end of World War II. Everyone, or almost everyone, is already aware of it. The institution of payola, the rigged quiz shows, white-collar employees matter-of-factly stealing from their corporate employers, the admittedly universal prevalence of cheating on exams, the evidence of proliferating corruption in the world of sports, teen-age behavior reaching "the point of alarm" as reported in Darien, Connecticut, last May —these and other circumstances make up such a clear pattern of deteriorated morals * that the New Testa-

* According to Webster's New World Dictionary, "moral" implies conformity with the generally accepted standards of

ment seems almost sentimental in depicting eleven apostles and one Judas. In our bailiwick, one cannot help thinking, the ratio would be reversed.

But perhaps a long view does not justify the concern which is being felt. Haven't we grown more tolerant? Today we treat children, criminals, unwed mothers, alcoholics, divorcees, compulsive Don Juans, etcetera, with much less cruelty than our forefathers did. This undeniable advance in civilized behavior, it could be argued, makes up for the slipshod morality which keeps appearing so consistently at the top of the news.

And so it would, if we were living in the same circumstances as our forebears. But in the earlier decades of this century, millions of people were kept on the straight and narrow path by hard work. It required so many hours of labor to earn a living as a streetcar conductor or to bring up a family without benefit of frozen foods, that corruption was more or less the prerogative of the rich. Today, however, toil and drudgery no longer operate among the population at large as moral stabilizers. Hence the need for a recognized and universally respected moral standard is greater than it used to be. But just at this moment when the need is greater, there seems to be a general collapse of ethical standards.

In 1960, *Look* sent out a dozen reporters to make a

---

goodness or rightness in conduct or character, and "ethical" implies conformity with an elaborated, ideal code of moral principles. This is the way the words will be used here.

survey of American morality all over the country, and published the results with a commentary by Walter Lippmann.

"America," said Lippmann, "is beginning to accept a new code of ethics that allows for chiseling and lying."

Chiseling and lying are not the most dramatic sins in the book, but they are two of the most important. Murder usually requires a special set of circumstances, but lying is, so to speak, available to everybody. To advertisers; to television celebrities like Charles Van Doren; to government itself.

According to the *Look* reporters, many interviewees felt that present-day Americans lie and condone lying in others (though still trying to teach their children to be truthful) because of the influence of Freud and Darwin. There is no longer a bearded personal God to punish wrong-doing. And it is certainly true that Freud and Darwin moved in on the theological landscape like a crew of bulldozers, and by the time they trundled off, there was not much left that was recognizable.

But Darwin was way back a hundred years ago and Freud came at the end of the nineteenth century. Surely there must have been more recent elements contributing to Lippmann's "new code of ethics." For instance, while there is no wide recognition of it, or perhaps no recognition at all, a number of liars have been structured into American life in the last decade and a half, notably in the field of public affairs, and there has been every indication that the society, taken by and large, approves of them. If it does not actually approve of their lying, it approves of them enough in other ways so that the untruthfulness is reduced to a mere peccadillo or forgivable eccentricity.

One such culturally assimilated liar was the now dead and presumably half-forgotten Whittaker Chambers.

At first glance it might seem that a writer must be not only outside the culture, but also pixilated, to revive—at a time when one horrible crisis follows another—the memory of the freakish Chambers, who died two years ago. But if we have a deteriorated morality, some kind of wrong turning must have started the downward process; and such a wrong turning would be in the past rather than in the present and would be something whose significance was not apparent at the time.

Incidentally, it should be said promptly that no consideration will be given at the moment to the guilt or innocence of Alger Hiss. The concern here is in quite another direction. Hiss was hoicked out of the society. What is to be considered here is the symbolic influence, possibly more long-lived than is suspected, of certain people the society retained and with apparent ease absorbed.

Only the importance of the hypothesis involved, only the necessity for some kind of insight into the collapsing morality, justifies bringing up the subject of Whittaker Chambers. Those old enough to remember him grow fewer every year, and even among them, there is no simple, single, clear-cut attitude about Chambers. Some people accept without question the picture Chambers himself paints in his autobiography, *Witness*, where he appears as a self-sacrificing patriot to whom the whole country is indebted because of his revelations about Communism in the State Department under Roosevelt. At the other end of the spectrum is a school of thought which, on the basis of his self-confessed perjuries, considers him to have been a pathological liar and a blot on American justice.

In between, and probably the largest group among those aware of the subject at all, are the people whose attitude toward Chambers is one of uneasy acceptance. These people would like nothing better than to pass on and forget him, and they in particular are likely to feel resistant to any interpretation of events in which he figures as an important and still significant social symbol. * But if the momentary discomfort can be borne of Chambers' ambiguity, a clearer insight into our life in recent years might eventually be forthcoming.

We have the word of one of his Columbia professors that Chambers as an undergraduate wrote bril-

---

* There is even a school of thought—some slight mention of it was made in the papers when he died—which holds that Chambers never at any time left the Communist Party and that in his career as a witness, he served its interests beautifully.

liant if morbid poetry; but the same professor is also reported to have said, "Whittaker just doesn't know when he is telling the truth." Even Richard Nixon, who was ultimately to make such political capital out of the Hiss case, was apparently slow to warm up to Chambers as a vessel of truth. In his column of October 28, 1957, Westbrook Pegler, writing enthusiastically about Robert Stripling, one-time counsel for the House Un-American Activities Committee, said:

"Political legend has it that Nixon turned up the pumpkin papers and thus, ultimately, sent Alger Hiss to prison. Actually, Stripling did the job long after Nixon had written off Whittaker Chambers as a melancholy freak unworthy of belief."

And according to Alistair Cooke, in *A Generation on Trial*, Nixon was in a frenzy of anxiety when the grand jury was hearing both Hiss and Chambers for fear the jurors would decide to indict Chambers first.

People who were reading headlines ten or fifteen years ago may remember Chambers' many self-contradictions and doublings back and forth when he came to testify under oath in court.

Hiss *did not/did* engage in espionage.

Hiss *did/did not* pay Communist Party dues to Chambers.

Chambers *had/had not* left the Party by the end of 1937. This last was a particularly crucial reversal since the papers he produced to back up his story were dated January to April, 1938.

That Chambers lacked the one quality which above all others should characterize a witness in a court of law, namely, truthfulness, was remarked upon by the Earl Jowitt, the late Lord Chancellor and former Attorney General of Great Britain, in his book, *The Strange Case of Alger Hiss.*

"Anybody may be excused for giving a story a 'new hat and stick,' if I may borrow the phrase from Sir Walter Scott," wrote this jurist, "but with Whittaker Chambers the desire to embroider and embellish is so transcendant that I do not believe he knows when he is leaving the straight and narrow path of truth."

Nevertheless, despite Chambers' repeated admissions of lying under oath, he appears to be the undislodgeable witness in our courts of law. Respectable men and respectable institutions accommodated themselves to his self-confessed perjury and to various other aspects of an eccentric persona which the burgesses of an earlier day might not have been able to tolerate. Chambers was assimilated by the culture *on his own terms* as a sober patriot and a responsible man.

To be sure, in an era of mass communications, true perspective often depends on not being misled by news "coverage." Alger Hiss, ironically enough, has remained through the years more "newsworthy" than Chambers. When Chambers died, in the summer of 1961, the press behaved oddly and uncharacteristically. The government's witness had been dead two days and was already cremated before the news was given to the papers. Yet the newsmen, who usually say they cannot fulfill their responsibility to the public without full and immediate access to events, accepted this straight-arming with the meekness of St. Cecilia at the organ and gave Chambers' death about the same amount of space they gave to the passing of Peaches Browning, which occurred at the same time.*

However, despite the fact that few people bothered to wave him good-by, it is Chambers who is integrated into the culture and not the Celebrated Defendant. Chambers was woven into the warp and woof of our society by publishers who competed fiercely for the chance to bring out what they judged, correctly, to be his highly profitable autobiography. He was woven into the fabric of American life by the *Saturday Evening Post*, which changed its cover format for the first time in many years in order to call attention to the fact that *Witness* was being serialized inside.

The Book-of-the-Month Club judges helped us to digest him, and so, too, did highly selective, kid-glove handling of his idiosyncrasies by journalists who are not usually kid-gloved about idiosyncratic behavior. He may also have been maintained in the posture of respectability by the fact that a second book he wrote was never published, despite the great success of the

* For the benefit of those unfamiliar with the newspaper sensations of the 1920's, Peaches Browning was a very young woman who was first adopted by an aging real estate man named Browning—which caused a lot of raised eyebrows—and who later married him. She called him Daddy and they were front-page news for a while.

first. The second manuscript, according to report, bordered on the pathological.

Time, one of whose senior editors Chambers was at the time of the trial, saw nothing incongruous in a news magazine being edited by a transcendant embroiderer and embellisher; and according to *Witness*, pensioned Chambers off handsomely when, of his own volition, he resigned. Finally, although not much note was taken of his passing elsewhere, *Life* gave him an obituary editorial which called him "lovable," and coupled him with Senator Borah as one of "a pair of great dissenters." And a year after he died, *Esquire* ran a glowingly adulatory feature article on "The Last Words of Whittaker Chambers," by William F. Buckley. (Incidentally, Buckley, by a curious Freudian slip, remarked in his piece that many people had not been able to make up their minds about *Chambers'* guilt or innocence!)

Thus was Chambers assimilated into our society. Highly visible enterprises endorsed him, *and those endorsements have not since been withdrawn. They still stand.*

It may be objected, of course, that society's accommodation to Whittaker Chambers was not total.

And, to be sure, it was not.

Many people with moral convictions were extremely unhappy about it. They had to keep telling themselves over and over again that Chambers was a necessary evil. He was a spy; he was a stool pigeon; he had had a sordid past; but we had to find out what had been going on in the State Department during the thirties.

However, Chambers was not promoted and sold to the general public as a necessary evil. He was not pictured to the country at large as a sorry instrument, but unfortunately the only one available, who had to be used in pursuit of "national security," and who would immediately be tossed upon the ethical junk heap when the nation's safety was guaranteed. Of course, the public could have been made aware of Chambers as a sorry instrument had he been indicted for perjury too, along with Hiss, but in that case it would probably have been impossible to indict Hiss. So, at least, Richard Nixon asserted in several press interviews late in 1948. Indicting Chambers, Nixon said, "would probably destroy the only opportunity to indict other individuals involved because the star witness will be an indicted and convicted person."

There were people—who can say how many?—whose ethical standards simply would not stretch to embrace Whittaker Chambers. But the whole force of the American government affirmed (and does to this day) that he was a believable witness; and especially after his autobiography started getting the celebrity treatment, people who could not adjust to him had to keep silent. Or, if they wished to communicate with the general public, they had to pretend to accept Chambers' respectability.

Journalists, sociologists, historians, ministers, teachers or politicians, regardless of their opinion about

Hiss, might have considered privately that the government's witness was, on the basis of his own asseverations, a sort of Idiot Boy of ethics. But to say any such thing in public was to bring down on one's head the immediate rebuke, "Are you daring to criticize the American jury system?" It can only be guesswork—there are no statistics—but it seems possible that many of the people who now live outside the culture had their first intimation of exile when they discovered that there was an Official Attitude toward Whittaker Chambers which could not be publicly challenged.

The rapid pace of world history, and the emergence of a new generation which did not live through the Hiss case as adults, have combined partially to obliterate the memory of Chambers. But if a commentator like Lippmann discerns "a new code of ethics" which accommodates to chiseling and lying, is it not pertinent to recall that—along with Freud and Darwin, and much closer to us in time—there is firmly affixed into our cultural heritage a notable palterer with the truth?

This is not, of course, to construct a devil-theory of history, with Whittaker Chambers as the devil. It is merely to bring to bear, upon a deteriorated morality, the kind of realism expressed by the English social critic Raymond Williams when he said, "Old images never die, they have to be publicly broken."

The difficulty in breaking the image of Chambers is that the necessity for it runs counter to a deeply held

American belief. This belief is seldom expressly stated, but it operates with all the force of tribal folklore. In a mass communications society, some such tenet or formulation is probably inevitable. Certainly many intelligent people entertain it, though sometimes quite unconsciously.

The belief is that a reprehensible character has a bad influence on the surrounding culture only for that period of time when he is getting a lot of publicity. Once the reprehensible fellow has dropped out of the headlines, once he has been reduced to obscurity by a whole new wave of dramatic events, any unfortunate effect he might have had on moral standards is more or less automatically sponged out.

Thus, even for people who were deeply disturbed by it at the time, the Hiss case eventually becomes just another journalistic phenomenon, one of the ephemeral "facts" of a preceding decade. The idea that the informer in that case, though long since out of the picture as a man, might as a symbol have a half-life as long as plutonium's is sure to be received with skepticism.

But what is not understood—perhaps because our culture is so popularity-obsessed—is that you do not have to admire a headliner to be influenced by him. A man may know that nothing in the world could have induced him to do as Charles Van Doren did, but by the time that man has lived through the saturative news and discussion which attended the scandal, he is nearer to behaving like Van Doren than he was before. Conduct which was formerly unthinkable and unfamiliar has become, if still unthinkable, at least familiar. Of two restraining factors, one has been dissolved, and although Van Doren ultimately joins Chambers in oblivion, the dissolved inhibition cannot be restored.

The question which today disturbs everybody, from the Reinhold Niebuhrs to the principals of public schools, is the question of declining moral standards. Could it be said that morality is, in a sense, like a garden pool? If you throw enough rocks into a pool, it will overflow and turn the surrounding greensward into a slippery and unlovely mess. Reprehensible characters, whether political like Whittaker Chambers and the late Senator McCarthy or non-political like Charles Van Doren, describe a trajectory and make a splash. Then they disappear from view. But once out of sight, they do not dissolve like some kind of giant-sized aspirin. They are still there, displacing the pure water and making the footing treacherous.

No single stone makes the pool overflow. It takes an accumulation of them. Richard Nixon, for instance, is probably a larger stone than Chambers. But Chambers more than anyone shows how, when a reprehensible man is in the headlines for any substantial period of time, the culture insensibly accommodates itself to his reprehensibility. When the man himself disappears, as he eventually does, *the accommodation remains.* Thus young people today who never heard of Whittaker Chambers are reacting in their various

ways to a moral climate which was keyed to Chambers'
shortcomings.

(It should be noted here that the operative phrase
is "for any substantial period of time." There are always transgressors in the news, whether they be cadets
at West Point who have cheated on exams, basketball
players who have accepted bribes, or conflict-of-interest
gentlemen like the late Harold Talbott, Eisenhower's
Secretary of the Air Force. But people like these come
and go too fast to make any profound impression on
the public mind. Of Charles Van Doren, on the other
hand, it was said when he tumbled from his pedestal
that more Americans knew his name than knew the
name of Eisenhower himself.)

In his role of reliable witness and virtuous man,
Headliner Chambers received the usual journalistic
and commercial exploitation. That exploitation had
the result of locking us into a Chambers climate of
morality from which we have not been freed to this
day.

The word "lock" is used advisedly. The usual belief
about our society is that it moves so fast and is so
incredibly flexible that people can barely keep their
footing in it. In terms of the destruction of old,
familiar landmarks and the invention of hovercraft to
take the place of automobiles, this belief is certainly
justified.

There is one way, however, in which American society is as rigid and static as Egyptian funerary art.
When an "image," in all its sentimentality, shallow-

ness and one-dimensional quality is once launched before the American public, that image freezes into a posture almost as changeless as Amenhotep with his hawk headdress and sideways-turned feet. What "public relations" has added up to, in sum, is that if ours is the Age of Anything, it is the Age of the One-Trait Personality. Thus Eisenhower is "genial," Perry Como is "relaxed," Dean Martin drinks, the late Marilyn Monroe was "sexy," Kennedy is "young," and Whittaker Chambers is a responsible man and a patriot.

Many dramatic events have intervened since the government's witness had his day in the limelight, but John Crosby once made an interesting point about the abiding influence of the seemingly transient.* Discussing a TV drama called "Two Tests on Tuesday," about a college student who cheated on exams, Crosby wrote:

The poor kid works in a parking lot to pay his way through college. That, plus his school work, means he gets only four hours' sleep a night. He is approaching the point of complete exhaustion. He has a wife and child. His whole future is tied up in whether he passes his exam or not.

So how can you fail to feel that the professor should pass him? But the trouble with this kind of playwriting is that it is unethical. A great many heroes—from Oedipus Rex to Hamlet—have had a bum shake from the outset; they have been put, by circumstances outside their control, into intolerable positions. Just the same, retribution caught up with them because it had to.

* New York *Herald Tribune* TV *Guide*, December 22–28, 1961.

This is the nature of tragedy. Society demands certain penalties for certain transgressions and when you make exceptions for whatever reasons—I am not speaking of the courts now but of dramatic works—you weaken the moral fabric of your play. And in every viewer there is a little weakening of his own moral fiber. All of us, from day to day, have to withstand temptations of some sort. If we see weakness condoned for whatever reason, it pulls the rug out from under the rest of us.

Crosby puts his finger on the cause of deteriorated morals when he speaks of making exceptions, and the instance of Whittaker Chambers shows how the degenerative process works.

In a time of great hysteria, the signal goes forth.

"It's all right to lie if you're uncovering Communists in the State Department."

Time passes, however, and has its usual eroding effect. Somewhere along the line the conditional clause gets lost. Fifteen years later we have "a new code of ethics" because the signal has been truncated and now says simply, "It's all right to lie."

III

———◦◦———

The Cuckoo's Egg

WHITTAKER CHAMBERS is only a springboard. The ultimate objective is to deal with larger considerations. For instance, not everybody agrees that "It's all right to lie." Some people—often those middle-aged or over, and sometimes young people, too, if we may believe what we read—are deeply troubled by the exceeding permissiveness that seems to have come over American life. These people look up from reading their books, magazines and newspapers and say helplessly, "The rules are changed."

And indeed the rules have been changed, for a usurpation has taken place in American life, a usurpation which has been going on for fifteen years and is now all but complete. Like the cuckoo laying its eggs in another bird's nest, a pseudo-ethic has taken the place once occupied by an older, traditional ethic. This pseudo-ethic is a false, twisted and deceptive code of behavior which, without explicitly saying so, defines good as that which maintains the one-institution society.

The false ethic has four major attributes:

It looks down rather than up for authority and sanction.

It is consistently vague and evasive and depends a great deal on communication-by-default.

It often holds up as desirable behavior what are in effect crazy inversions of the traditional ethic it has supplanted.

It is indissolubly linked to, and could not exist without, anti-Communism as a domestic issue.

The older, traditional ethic, to which the term "Judeo-Christian" is usually applied, will be discussed at length in the next chapter. For the moment, we need consider it only in order to contrast the manner in which it derives authority with the manner in which the false ethic derives sanction and authority.

Any standard of ethics must be backed up by some kind of sanction, or people would feel it was weightless and trivial, and ignore it. The older, traditional ethic looks upward for the sanction that makes it impressive in people's eyes. The new pseudo-ethic looks downward.

For religious believers, the authority of the traditional ethic derives from God Himself. For nonbelievers, the sanction for the ethic still comes, as it were, from on high, for it derives from the lives and teachings of superior people. It derives from such strong figures as Christ in the New Testament and Moses and Isaiah in the old. It derives from men like Abraham Lincoln or St. Francis of Assisi or Martin Luther. It derives from writers like Shakespeare and Goethe and Balzac. It derives from philosophers and thinkers like Socrates and Aristotle.

The list could be extended, but the point is simple. For believer and nonbeliever alike, the common note is superiority. The authority and weight and impressiveness of the older, traditional ethic—the quality which makes people respect it and try to live up to it— stems from the superior vision of the prophets, the superior gifts and insights of the great teachers, or, for the believer, the actual perfection of godhead itself.

The pseudo-ethic, on the other hand, looks for its authority and force and impressiveness in exactly the opposite direction. As one might expect in a society with mass communications and mass markets, the pseudo-ethic says in effect that whatever is popular, is right. Where the traditional ethic derives its sanction from the superiority of a few, the pseudo-ethic derives its sanction from the inferiority of a great many. The pseudo-ethic is keyed, not to the spiritually gifted, but to the spiritually ungifted. They, by the sheer mass of their numbers, give the pseudo-ethic that stature—in the eyes of a majority of present-day Americans—

which the traditional ethic derived from examples set by outstanding men.

Under the aegis of the false ethic, the inch-high moral hurdle which is all the drugged television addict can scale becomes the new criterion of virtue. The Ten Commandments (Thou shalt not steal—Thou shalt not bear false witness), while not openly and specifically abandoned, are tacitly by-passed in favor of the more agreeable dictum that Charles Van Doren only did what anybody else would have done.

The traditional ethic gets its authority (with those for whom it has authority) from a few strong figures representing certain moral principles. The pseudo-ethic, in exactly opposite fashion, gets its authority from a great many weak ones representing none. Thus, in terms of the pseudo-ethic, any action which a "nation-wide" audience can be persuaded to condone becomes an acceptable action, no matter what Abraham Lincoln would have thought of it.

William H. Whyte, Jr., touched upon this debased ethical authority in *The Organization Man*, when he noted with fastidious disapproval the growth of what he called "the social ethic." According to the social ethic, one finds out what is the right thing to do by looking at what the other people in the peer group are doing—the bowling club at Levittown, the research team in the laboratory, and so on. But Whyte's name for this procedure is misleading, for by calling it "the social ethic," he seems to suggest it is a weakened form of the Judeo-Christian ethic. However, Whyte's social ethic is not a weakened form of the traditional ethic; it is the *exact opposite* of the Judeo-Christian ethic. There is nothing in the social ethic—Whyte did not seem to realize this—that would keep you from joining a lynch mob. In fact, according to the social ethic, you would be *obliged* to join the lynch mob.

The supplanting of the Judeo-Christian ethic by the new pseudo-ethic has been a gradual process, but occasionally certain events have given the usurpation a big shove forward. One such event was Richard Nixon's "Checkers" speech of the 1952 campaign. The "Checkers" speech can now be seen, with the advantage of hindsight, to have been much more than the simple matter of a politician getting himself off a hot spot. The triumph enjoyed by that oration implanted in millions of American minds a major canon of the pseudo-ethic: namely, that few actions are so bad that they cannot become acceptable or even good through "popularity."

When the New York *Post* originally broke the story that Nixon, while in Congress, had accepted eighteen thousand dollars from a group of California businessmen, the first, instantaneous reaction of press and public was in terms of the traditional ethic. Eisenhower was reported to be furious, and there was general agreement that Nixon was finished. But hours passed, and even days. The Vice-Presidential candidate did not withdraw from the race, and Eisenhower made no statement condemning his running mate's action and affirming the traditional ethic. Soon, from the significant silence of the leaders and top men, people began to get the hint of how they were supposed to think. Then the political journalists, followed by the general public, changed from the simple, spontaneous pronouncement that Nixon was finished to the tentative, equivocal question, "What will he do now?"

What he did is well known. He went before a vast television audience whose size had probably been considerably augmented by the inaction and suspense which preceded the hero's appearance. He made a speech which was a tissue of evasions, side-steppings and specious sentimentalities and wound up begging his viewers to wire the Republican National Committee and tell him what to do. According to Earl Mazo's biography of Nixon:

Telephone and telegraph lines were clogged across the land. Despite Nixon's plea that messages go to the National Committee, they were sent to everything that sounded Republican—from the Eisenhower train to local political clubs—and the sentiment seemed almost unanimous: "Keep Nixon."

Mr. Mazo further says that although the messages were never totaled, Party headquarters in Washington alone got three hundred thousand letters, cards, telegrams and petitions, signed altogether by a million people.

Eisenhower embraced his running mate, called him a "warrior," said he had "courage," and addressed him as "my boy." The campaign continued with its cast of characters unchanged.

The Democrats, of course, were outraged on both political and moral grounds, but even the most sensitive moralist did not perceive what a leg-up the Californian, in his nervous scramble for self-preservation, had given to the new pseudo-ethic.

"Hypocrisy," La Rochefoucauld said cynically, "is the homage that vice pays to virtue."

Nixon's achievement showed that this kind of tribute need no longer be paid, since vice, properly handled, can *become* virtue. Proper handling consists of winning the applause of a vast audience, for they in their anonymous millions, rather than identified men of proven worth, have become the arbiters of what is right and what is wrong.

In every beginner's art appreciation class, the students are told that in a picture, the space between two objects is just as important to the eye as the objects themselves. Similarly, a social environment is just as much made up of what *isn't there* as of the things people actually experience. An outstanding characteristic of the false ethic has been that it developed and revealed itself to the American public mostly by inference and implication instead of by positive assertion and unmistakable action. Negatives, omissions, silences and things left undone all contributed in a major way to build it up.

After the market crash of 1929 and the subsequent economic depression, it was the American consensus that this tragic dislocation of people's lives should not be allowed to recur, and to that end the Securities and Exchange Commission was set up. But after the hysteria known as McCarthyism seemed to have run its course, though there was wide agreement that the phenomenon had been a national disgrace, no one suggested that a political equivalent of the SEC be put into operation so that the disgrace would not recur.

The witch-hunting period showed us that a revision of old rules or a passage of new ones is needed, if the private citizen called before a Congressional committee is not to risk all the punitive force of court action while at the same time being afforded none of its protections. The House Un-American Activities Committee and the Senate Internal Security Sub-Committee have no sanction for questioning private individuals save for the purpose of passing necessary legislation; and some kind of automatic termination is clearly necessary for Congressional investigation if it fails to come up with legislative proposals after a reasonable period of interrogation. But despite the deep shock which many people felt about McCarthyism, the ordinary common sense of preventive medicine has been conspicuous by its absence.

Once you become aware of them, the lacunae and the significant nonoccurrences mount up. The discovery of Charles Van Doren's collusion with the quiz show riggers produced great excitement of a shallow, superficial kind and a huge, blurred mumble of ethical fudging and moral equivocation. But the healthy outrage of a self-respecting public, aware of its own worth and of what was due it, was lacking. A few angry voices spoke out sternly here and there—not many—but it was to be a year before, as quietly as a mouse in sneakers, the society he had so successfully gulled indicted the former celebrity and his fellow sinners for perjury.

Again, when traditional moral standards demanded the dismissal of Sherman Adams, Eisenhower exclaimed, "But I need him!" and Adams continued as Presidential assistant for many weeks after it was discovered that he had accepted gifts from Bernard Goldfine. The Presidential assistant concluded his public career, after his delayed resignation, by writing a book of memoirs, rights to which were purchased for a high price by *Life*. That magazine printed Adams' reminiscences in two extended articles in January and June, 1961. And by the fall of 1962, the Adams fall from grace had been sufficiently lost sight of, through not being mentioned, for a college in the Middle West to invite him to give a series of three lectures on politics and public life.

A notable and important non-event, in terms of the moral climate, was Eisenhower's failure to defend his friend and benefactor, General Marshall, against Senator McCarthy. The failure, too, of almost the entire press to call its soldier-hero to account for the betrayal was the sort of omission which materially helped the growth of the false ethic.

This inertness and absence of reaction contrasts sharply with the vital, defiant and clearly defined be-

havior which has its wellsprings in the older ethic—
such behavior, for instance, as that of Lillian Hellman
and Arthur Miller in refusing to "name names" for a
Congressional committee; or of the white clergyman in
New Orleans who led a Negro child by the hand past
an angry mob and into school; or of the actor George
C. Scott who refused to be nominated for an Oscar
because of the vulgarity and phoniness of the compe-
tition; or of the people who picketed Kirsten Flagstad,
when she sang at Carnegie Hall, for having gone to
Nazi Germany and sung for Goering; or of Dorothy
Day, editor of the *Catholic Worker*, who has sub-
mitted to numberless arrests in protest against civil
defense and nuclear war.

"The fog comes on little cat feet."

The protests that are never voiced, the halt that is
never called, the clearly deserved punishment that is
never meted out, the self-discipline that is weakly and
wordlessly evaded, the note of criticism that is
not sounded—what all these add up to, so far as a
general public is concerned, is communication-by-
default.

Present-day America, with its vacuum tube and
giant printings, must be by all odds the most verbal
society this planet has ever seen, and yet ironically
enough some of the American public's most strongly
implanted attitudes have been brought about through
communication-by-default. When Eisenhower consistently failed to do his homework and spent at least two
afternoons a week playing golf at Burning Tree, he

suggested to a huge population, and without ever saying a word, that being a head of state in a hydrogen-
bomb world is a mere run-of-the-mill employment
like being city-wide chairman of the Community
Chest. (How distorting communication-by-default can
be was shown by the fact that Eisenhower's successor
was hailed as virtually another Pericles, by some sections of press and public, merely because he was able
to do a day's work for a day's pay.)

Kennedy makes a great to-do about things cultural,
and in his soirées at the White House he uses up
artists as if they were Kleenex; * but the President's
failure to educate a painfully ignorant electorate on
issues like disarmament or poverty in Latin America
conveyed one strong, clear message to that electorate—
namely, that nobody need worry about any wrenching,
disruptive pains of growth or rude shoves in the direction of maturity, because when President Kennedy
talks about the United States getting off dead center,
he does not really mean it.

Public relations and the creation of "images" is so
much a part of everyone's thinking in America that
communication-by-default is not generally recognized
as a way of getting in touch with people. But it is an

---

* Since the President has to entertain, it is better for him
to have Pablo Casals than Mickey Mouse. But a President's
primary concern should be the political rather than the artistic
education of the public, and certainly the artistic should not
be made, as it has been in the Kennedy administration, *to
take the place of* the political.

effective method of putting a message across, as the present level of American morality shows.

When, in the bomb-shelter excitement of 1961, Christian ministers—a few only, of course—said that it was morally permissible to shoot the neighbors in the doorway of your shelter, the false ethic probably reached some kind of apogee. But the pseudo-ethic was well established before the bomb-shelter issue arose and continued to flourish after it died away. The shelter-doorway ukase, however, illustrates another important characteristic of the false ethic—namely, that its moral pronouncements are frequently crazy inversions of the Judeo-Christian ethic it has supplanted.

All through the codification of this new formula for American behavior (to the extent that it is codified at all), runs a feeling of things stood on their heads. The pseudo-ethic says you may shoot your neighbor in the doorway of the bomb shelter, *without sacrificing your right to be called a decent human being,* whereas the older ethic says, "Love thy neighbor as thyself" and "Greater love hath no man than this, that he lay down his life for his friend."

The shelter-doorway pronouncement shows the false ethic at its most garish, but other instances of its crazy invertedness are more immediately realistic and closer to home.

Harry Truman, twenty years ago, made a remark that illustrates the genuine ethic. Truman was at that time chairman of a Congressional committee investigating government contracts—a committee which was said to have saved the taxpayers fifteen billion dollars. The ex-President said almost *en passant* that his staff had been extremely careful in the material it released to the newspapers because it wished to be sure that no innocent citizens were maligned. The Truman statement illustrates simply and pellucidly the older, traditional ethic, one of whose most basic premises is that a man is innocent until proven guilty.

It comes instantly to mind that in the field of politics, this premise has been stood on its head. The McCarthy accusations, the way in which the treason trials were conducted and the Congressional investigations of people's long-dead politics taught a vast section of the American public to consider that a person accused of "Communism" is guilty unless he can prove himself innocent. Indeed, it is probably not an exaggeration to say that with some of the more uninformed levels of the populace, a person so charged can never prove himself innocent, no matter what he does.

The idea that a man is innocent until proved guilty is one of the most mature and civilized parts of Anglo-Saxon law, and human passions being as unruly as they are, sometimes one of the most difficult to give effect to. The American press may take a large share of the blame for saddling us with the pseudo-ethic in the field of political opinion. The press printed as the top of the news every single accusation of disloyalty and conspiracy that had the slightest tinge of drama or sensationalism, no matter how discredited the accuser or how honorable and reputable the victim. The justification for such an extended airing—it went on for years—of unproven charges was that, "The people have the right to know." This rationale is a complete inversion of the press's own professional and ethical ideal of "hard news," according to which you do not print that Paris has fallen to the Germans merely on the say-so of the Germans. You first check with other sources.

As a result of journalistic intemperance, we now have an American public of which wide sections feel that where any kind of left-wing belief is involved, injustice is not only forgivable, but is even a little bit better, as a goal, than justice itself.

Many instances testify to the crazy invertedness which the new pseudo-ethic has brought into American morality.

"Touch pitch," says the traditional ethic, "and ye shall be defiled."

In the early fifties, however, the late Senator Robert A. Taft demonstrated to American newspaper readers that it is entirely possible to touch pitch and suffer no defilement at all.

Even the liberals who spent all their time battling his rock-ribbed conservatism were wont to speak admiringly of Senator Taft as an incorruptibly honest man. But on March 22, 1952, the Ohio Senator—tempted beyond his strength, perhaps, by Presidential yearnings—endorsed the activities of Senator McCarthy.

"Keep talking," Taft said to the Senator from Wisconsin, "and if one case doesn't work out, proceed with another."

Taft's defection from the ranks of the incorruptibly honest passed almost without comment, the public prints and organs of opinion, save for a very few, tending to shrug it off. And when the Senator died, in 1953, his body lay in state in the rotunda of the Capitol, a distinction only rarely accorded; the obituaries vied with each other in calling him "honorable"; and so mummified has his One-Trait Personality since become that Joseph Alsop, writing in 1959, called him "one of the biggest and finest men of his generation." Senator Taft forfeited his honor, and so far as the average newspaper reader knows, never did anything to retrieve it, but his honorableness has become one of the Ritual Lies of the Establishmentarians.

Perhaps it does not seem important. The inflated reputation is nothing new, and Time is unsparing of it. But one cannot help speculating on the social role of words. If the word "honorable" is applied to Senator Taft, what word is left for the man who, tempted as Taft was tempted, manages to resist the temptation? One thinks of George Washington's delicate sense of honor, and of the authors of the Declaration of Independence pledging "our lives, our fortunes and our sacred honor." If the society has no word for the man who resists the temptation, does it not soon wind up being unable to produce him?

Actually, there was for some people a kind of horror

in the comparative silence and lack of comment which greeted Taft's endorsement of McCarthy. It was as if someone had dropped a tray of ice cubes on a marble floor and it had landed without producing the slightest clatter, jingle or tinkle.

Popular novelists like Herman Wouk, Allen Drury or Sloan Wilson and popular nonfiction writers of the school of Vance Packard and Martin Mayer all seem to arrive, in their books, at the same conclusion— namely, that life in consumer-oriented America, while disadvantageous in some important respects, should nevertheless be faced with cheerful resignation. In dramatic and shocking contrast, some of the more serious artists and literary or social critics—people like Paul Goodman, Harvey Swados, Irving Howe, Kenneth Boulding, Kenneth Rexroth, Maxwell Geismar, Erich Fromm, Nelson Algren, the late C. Wright Mills, etcetera—speak in terms of total rejection. They are of one voice in using words like irrational, insane and lunatic to describe present-day American life, with its worship of waste in a world of starving continents and its trigger-happy readiness for a war which even the Pentagon admits would produce at least eighty million American dead.

Perhaps the sensation of distortion, of an environment impossible to identify with or relate to, which is felt by those who are outside the culture comes from the fact that so many of the moral pronouncements of the pseudo-ethic are crazy inversions of the Judeo-Christian ethic whose place it has taken. We all know from our own nightmares that the ultimate chill of horror comes, not from things totally strange and never seen before, but from distortions of the familiar. Thus the really visceral, sickening shock of fright is not evoked by creatures from outer space, but from such human sights as the soldiers with the unspeakable face wounds that the French in World War I called *"les gueules cassées."*

Distortion of the familiar.

The traditional ethic has not disappeared. It is still here, but it has been crazily inverted and its miry ankles thrash the air where its head ought to be.

In a piece called "Time for a New Politics" in the May 26, 1962, issue of *The Nation,* Carey McWilliams wrote:

In no single respect is the obsolescence of the liberal-conservative dialogue quite so striking as in our national obsession with the so-called "Communist" problem in domestic politics. This alleged issue has been investigated at every level, state, federal and local, and in every walk of life, law, science, the ministry, education, the military, labor, industry, the arts, entertainment, the mass media— not once but again and again. Enough political energy has been dissipated in its pursuit to move mountains and modernize Africa. It has been "exposed" ad nauseam—in the press, in books, in pamphlets, over the radio, on TV, in motion pictures, sermons, lectures, seminars, mass meetings, "schools," etcetera. The phoniness of the issue has been ridiculed and satirized so often, and so widely, that our obsession with it has become an international stock joke. . . .

The American consensus on communism is so massive that the issue is not debatable; there is no "opposition" to debate it. The fact is that we debate only the degree of hatred that all proper Americans are expected to exhibit when the subject is mentioned. . . . If there was ever a phony issue, this is it. Yet in volume and weight it remains by all odds the most massive one in American politics—undebated, unchallenged and meaningless.

One can quarrel with nothing McWilliams says save his final word, "meaningless." The massive consensus of which he speaks is far from meaningless, for the fourth and by no means the least important aspect of the false ethic is that it is indissolubly linked to, and could not exist without, anti-Communism as a domestic issue.

A few years ago, shortly after alleged gamblers had been arrested in the Anastasia headquarters in Brooklyn, the late Anthony Anastasia was interviewed on television. Anastasia was all injured innocence and at one point burst out indignantly, "I'm anti-Communist! What more do they want of me?"

Before laughing too heartily at Brooklyn's Little Shepherd of Kingdom Come, it might be a good idea to look at what has been going on among his betters as the pseudo-ethic influences American reactions more and more.

"Frightened people in a score of desperate countries want to be on the winning but not necessarily the moral side; and we have to start winning soon."

So wrote Eric Sevareid in the backwash of the Cuban invasion.

Similarly, only a week after Ross Barnett, James Meredith and the riots at the University of Mississippi had monopolized the headlines, columnist William Shannon could proclaim:

"The fundamental reason why our bases are justified and Russian bases are not justified is that we stand for what is good in the world and the Russians stand for what is evil."

One could hardly ask for a clearer expression of the pseudo-ethic. We will be good only when it is convenient, but we will insist at all times on being *called* good. Ironically enough, the sentiments expressed grow logically out of Nixon's "Checkers" speech. As invoked by these liberal writers, the standard to be lived up to is not truthfulness, or fair play, or just conduct. The standard, apparently, is that anything done by us *becomes* good—even starting a nuclear war—and good is defined, not as something universal and having to do with all mankind, but by implication as whatever maintains our one-institution society.

The pseudo-ethic owes much of its evasiveness and slipperiness to the fact of its being keyed in with the so-called fight against Communism. This last phrase is so mercilessly overused in the United States that one cannot get through an ordinary day without reading or hearing it at least once and more probably several times. Reiteration, however, does not establish the truth of a reference—in fact, it is likely to indicate a Ritual Lie—and although we have soldiers fighting in Vietnam, here at home there *isn't* any fight against Communism.

In affluent, opulent, agreeable America, who fights?

You cannot have a fight without fighters.* The very word "controversial," however, applied to a fellow-citizen, sends Americans running for the storm cellars, and commentators of every stripe agree that the trend of American life is toward an increasingly bland emulsification. Indeed, the President, by forebearing to risk in churlish conflict any smallest part of his "popularity," has unwittingly indicated that despite an outward briskness, he is much more the captive of his environment than the commander of it. Save for a small but gallant peace movement, there is only one fight with really big stakes going on in America today, and that is the fight being waged by Negroes in pursuit of first-class citizenship.

That the "fight against Communism" does not exist —here at home, at any rate—is easily demonstrable.

All the resources of American society, and they are massive, are mobilized to make Americans product-

* A distinction must be made between fighters and haters. There are those among us who never tire of proclaiming that they hate Communism, but under calm scrutiny it looks more as if they just hate, period. When you turn the medal over and ask what they love, you do not find them among the Freedom Riders. You do not even find them passionately affirming that everyone ought to give up Havana cigars in order to embarrass Fidel Castro. A hater is not the same thing as a fighter.

minded. The economy as currently set up demands
this kind of orientation, and Americans have one of
their worst areas of Amenhotep rigidity when it comes
to the notion of reshaping the economy. Product-
minded we are, and product-minded we must be, almost everyone is agreed. And it is just not humanly
possible to be product-minded and fight-minded at
one and the same time. The two orientations require
completely opposite, and mutually exclusive, sets of
qualities. To be fight-minded, whether the enemy is
puerperal fever, the German Army, human slavery or
litterbugs, requires that people be intense, concen-
trated, pugnacious and, some might say, not without a
streak of savagery. To be product-minded requires that
people be relaxed (or you could also say "slack"),
diffused and agreeable (or uncritical, if you want to
put it that way).

America is currently product-minded; and nothing
shows up more clearly the falsity of the pseudo-ethic
than the fact that its exponents—who are, of course,
not conscious of being its exponents—use an alleged
fight which is not taking place as an excuse for letting
down the ethical bars. In the vague, cloudy background of the pseudo-ethic, there is presumably a
stark, desperate, "military" situation which makes it
necessary to jettison such distracting goals as scrupu-
lous honesty, fair play and simple justice.

Not, of course, that these higher ideals are to be
permanently given up. Public opinion, even in a mass
society, would never stand for that. They are merely

to be relegated to some unspecified future time when we are not in a "fight." But a supposedly postponed idealism is in reality an idealism that has already been discarded. The pseudo-ethic governs our lives, protected by the myth of a "fight against Communism" from the kind of scrutiny which would quickly show it up. The result can be no more succinctly expressed than in a sentence from one of Dwight Macdonald's essays.

"The uneasiness the Victorians felt in the presence of the base," wrote this critic, "we feel in the presence of the noble."

In a later chapter this speculation will consider whether there might have been something lying at the very roots of our society which gave rise to the pseudo-ethic and insured its triumph over the older, traditional ethic. A few preliminaries, however, will be necessary—first, to look at the Judeo-Christian ethic and determine whether, in losing it, we really lost anything of value; and second, to assess the role of General Eisenhower, "man of good will," in bringing about its downfall.

IV

The Ethic and the Nylon Savior

SOME YEARS AGO Sir Sacheverell Sitwell appeared on an American television show called "Wisdom," and the interviewer asked him, among other questions, why he didn't write a novel.

The Englishman smiled wryly.

"In these times," he said, "it would be like trying to play chess in an earthquake."

We live in a daunting world, full of terrifying novelties; and against such a background, discussing the Judeo-Christian ethic—for instance, "Sell what thou hast and give to the poor"—seems a little like playing chess in an earthquake.

Furthermore, since we are all by now accustomed to the lax, tolerant pseudo-ethic, the older code of conduct is likely to sound to many contemporary ears bad-tempered and unpleasantly militant. The pseudo-ethic, for example, finds one of its most characteristic expressions in the seemingly modest query, "Who am I to say what's right and wrong?" The traditional ethic, on the other hand, avers that saying what is right and wrong constitutes a normal responsibility of the mature adult.

"So far as my observation goes," wrote Joseph Wood Krutch in the Spring 1962 issue of *The American Scholar*, "neither the child, the adolescent nor the adult is likely to become a good or civilized man unless positive pressures (sometimes including deliberate punishment) are put upon him."

Positive pressures and deliberate punishment are not highly esteemed in the current American climate; and yet one has only to think about the purpose of ethics to see that they are far from being the tight-lipped affair that the general public, in its present lotus-eating state of mind, supposes.

Ethics provide stability. Reduced to its simplest terms, the existence of an ethic is what enables the host to go into the kitchen and fix drinks in the comfortable certainty that his guests will not, during his absence, take money from his wallet. Furthermore, although in the popular mind an ethic is a puritanical, ramrod-stiff set of injunctions, in actual practice a grounding in ethics makes people more flexible, for it lets them respond to new situations with confidence in their own characters. Finally, the ethic is the built-in, automatic control that takes over in moments of great stress, even panic, when all else in the personality has been temporarily shaken loose.

For all these reasons, therefore, it seems relevant in a world of flux and mortal peril to discuss the Judeo-Christian code of conduct.

It was a simple enough matter to define the false ethic in a single sentence; but the older, traditional ethic is too many-faceted to be compressed summarily into so small a compass. Way back in the 1920's, Norman Douglas, author of *South Wind*, described Christianity as "that quaint Alexandrian tutti-frutti"; and the complexity which evoked this mocking phrase about the religion is equally an aspect of the Judeo-Christian ethic. It takes a strong, unwearied intellect to sort out and make sense of the contradictions and inconsistencies which have developed in that ethic during the many centuries it has been in use. Perhaps a brief mention of a few of the many vicissitudes it has been through should precede any effort to define it.

In the course of its long history, the older, traditional ethic has often been attacked. It was open to attack because, unlike the silently evasive pseudo-ethic, it was *there*. Commands and directives whose meaning was usually unmistakable formed its body and substance.

"Lay not up for yourselves treasures on earth."

"*Honi soit qui mal y pense.*"

"Blessed are the meek."

"He who comes into equity must come with clean hands."

"Thou shalt not commit adultery."

"It isn't cricket."

"Whatsoever ye do even unto the least of these, ye do also unto Me."

Because of its specificity, critics could get at the traditional ethic, and they often did. Originators and explorers, opening up new ways of thought, could make some of its cardinal tenets look antiquated and absurd.

"Honor thy father and mother," runs the Biblical injunction, and everyone knows what mincemeat Freud made of that!

Consider also, "Money is the root of all evil."

Not only Christianity and Judaism, but every great religion in the world has made this affirmation repeatedly; but we now have for the first time in man's history whole societies so well off as to have earned the adjective, "affluent." We are also witnessing the so-called revolution of rising expectations, in which hundreds of millions of formerly exploited colonial peoples are demanding decent food and clothing. It would scarcely be appropriate for Westerners to talk to these populations about the desirability of wearing hair shirts.

A further complexity of the Judeo-Christian ethic is that large parts of it have traditionally been concerned with controlling and directing man's sex drive. From the Biblical woman taken in adultery—through the chastity belts, Mariolatry and the virility-dampening institution of chivalry in the Middle Ages—to the Puritans of Hawthorne's *The Scarlet Letter* and the Victorian Mrs. Grundy, the traditional ethic has been associated in people's minds with prohibitions about sex. However, the improved status of women in modern times, plus the development of contraceptives, have made most of the sexual mandates seem primitive.

Indeed, Robert Ardrey in his book, *African Genesis*, has given popular circulation to the idea that a stronger and more imperious instinct than sex, in the human animal, is the instinct to occupy and defend territory. This theory has by no means won general acceptance, but it serves at least to illustrate how new ideas, if they are widely taken up, can make important aspects of the traditional ethic suddenly irrelevant.

Other reversals, digressions and changes of emphasis in the ethic have been slow rather than sudden. New social classes develop and emerge in a society without reference to the society's ethic, and then the ethic has to find something to say about them. In *Religion and the Rise of Capitalism*, the late R. H. Tawney showed how the Protestant Reformation, seemingly a flight from the tyranny of Rome, was actually a process of modifying the traditional ethic to meet the needs of a rising merchant class.

During the Reformation, as Tawney pointed out in his classic work, the prudential virtues of thrift and industry were upgraded and became much more important than they had been in medieval Europe. Collecting interest, once the "sin" of usury, became respectable; and early-Christian notions of mortifying the flesh were played down in favor of the new idea that making money was actually virtuous. A basic ethical principle about money was modified during the Reformation, and tens of millions of people were slaughtered in religious wars and in extirpations of "heresy" so that the rule of poverty could be supplanted by the rule of prosperity.

There seems no end to the vicissitudes through which the older, traditional ethic has passed. In the nineteenth century, it derived a good deal of vitality from a widespread belief in the perfectibility of man. Since then, however, we have seen the Nazis murder six million Jews and, for political and ethnic reasons, several million other people. This civilized development was accompanied by two world wars of unprecedented carnage; and World War III now seems to be in the making. For most people, the optimistic Victorian belief in man's progress has become absurd.

Despite pessimism, however, the traditional ethic may yet have more life in it than seems possible. The Bible says that the poor we have always with us, but mankind has actually reached a point—just as unprecedented as the world wars, but in reverse—where it would be physically possible to wipe poverty from the face of the earth. G. K. Chesterton, writing in his life of Dickens about the savagery and brutality of the era in which the novelist grew up, remarked that "this 'hard and cruel' age was, after all, the age of reform. The gibbet stood up black above them; but it was black against the dawn." The dawn to which Chesterton referred was the French Revolution. In our day it may be the development of the world state.

Faith and loss of faith in progress is only one of many ups and downs in the history of the Western ethic. Society moves on more than one front at a time; and not only the advertising men, but also the social scientists, have struck blows at the Judeo-Christian ethic. In the second quarter of our century, the psychologists and anthropologists seemed for a while to have given the traditional ethic its *coup de grâce*, when they came up with the theory of ethical relativism.

According to this concept, undeniably fascinating when it was first introduced, behavior was to be judged in whatever context it was found, and the Hopi Indian in the desert of New Mexico was not to be compared in terms of right and wrong with people living in New York City. Thus the Kwakiutl Indians of the Northwest, whose custom it was to stage banquets that were orgies of meaningless display and senseless present-giving, could be regarded as in effect occupying the same moral level as Thorstein Veblen, Henry Thoreau and St. Paul.

But ethical relativism led to nowhere in particular, and like a rushing brook losing itself in a swamp, it eventually petered out. Perhaps the last word on it was said, somewhat tangentially, by Romain Gary in his memoir, *Promise at Dawn*. M. Gary described his mother's fierce devotion to him and dismissed with Gallic insouciance the notion that her affection might have been Oedipal. Incest, M. Gary remarked, seems unimportant in a hydrogen-bomb world, and so far as protection of the race is concerned, the taboo that has operated from time immemorial against parents and children seducing each other had better be invoked— in all its monolithic forbiddingness—against the use of nuclear weapons.

The older, traditional ethic has had a checkered and variable history and at best it can only be said to limp along. The Old Testament is a byword for harshness. The New Testament grew out of a slaves' religion and is in places committed to a meekness not normal for free men. It is said that Confucius was once told about the idea, picked up five hundred years later by the Christians, of recompensing injury with kindness, and the Eastern sage replied in practical vein, "With what, then, will you recompense kindness? Repay injury with justice and kindness with kindness."

What, then, does the Judeo-Christian ethic, that battered list of Thou-shalts and Thou-shalt-nots, add up to?

Is it something whose current eclipse by the pseudo-ethic is cause for dismay?

It may be that the older, traditional ethic has been supplanted by the new, false ethic because it *deserves* to be supplanted. That traditional ethic was distinguished, as Herbert J. Muller says, by the fact of its prophets being notable among the religious leaders of mankind for the eloquence of their protests against social injustice. But the argument might be made that, since we now have the affluent society and the welfare state, social injustice has been more or less done away with, save for occasional pockets here and there, and hence an ethic whose prophets are eloquent about it has become obsolete.

At least in the so-called developed countries.

All through the long history of the Judeo-Christian ethic, one note persists. The most consistent and reiterative emphasis seems to be on the importance of the individual, whether it is Job in the Old Testament saying, "Though He slay me, yet will I love Him; *but I will walk in mine own ways before Him,*" or the Bill of Rights in the American Constitution, which says in effect that the individual shall not be forbidden to, or punished for, walking in his own ways.

Nobody is to be regarded as expendable. For any reason at all. That, when all the contradictions and variations have been allowed for (the Chosen People, Saint Augustine's doctrine of infant damnation), would appear to be the deepest and most central meaning of the older, traditional ethic. To describe it in a single sentence: The Judeo-Christian ethic is a code of conduct in which good is defined as that which promotes, protects or enhances respect for the individual. This code, lived up to, produces as a sort of by-product what is usually called social justice—i.e., the equalization of advantage.

The question of whether, when we lost this ethic, we lost anything of value can be quickly answered. One has only to think of the situations in which respect for the individual is nonexistent.

In his autobiography, *Journey to the Beginning*, the reporter Edgar Snow tells of visiting Maidanek after the war and asking a janitor he found there what he, the janitor, thought about Maidanek's gruesome distinction of having once gassed eighteen thousand people in a single day.

The janitor, Snow reported, looked at him with wrinkled forehead.

"But they were guilty," he said.

People of middle age or older can perhaps still remember the disbelieving horror many Americans felt in 1932–33 when the Soviet government, under Stalin, deliberately allowed four million people to starve to death during a famine in the Ukraine, in order to break the resistance to collective farming.

Apartheid in South Africa and McCarthyism in the United States are both situations in which respect for the individual is abrogated.

Nor has social injustice disappeared, even in the "developed" countries. It has merely taken on different forms. Planned obsolescence and nuclear testing do not represent social justice and the challenge of automation cannot possibly be met in orderly fashion save in terms of respect for the individual.

Admittedly, the Judeo-Christian ethic is a hodge-podge. Some parts of it have had to change, in the light of new conditions or man's advancing knowledge, but other parts, like the Golden Rule, endure. These enduring parts even find social and political expression in great concepts of Anglo-Saxon law or in representative government or the United Nations. If on the one hand the traditional ethic is associated with religious slaughters, the cruelties of Calvinism and the idiocy of smelly monks sitting for years on pillars, it has on the other been the matrix which nourished such figures as Franklin Roosevelt and Tolstoy. Most important of all, the need for its disciplines and its supportive qualities, alike, has never been more apparent than in America today, when so many people are living without them.

This much having been said, only one more aspect of the traditional ethic remains to be noted, but it is a crucial one—namely, that *the older, traditional ethic cannot be combined with the new pseudo-ethic.* No workable compromise is possible. There can be sanction-from-above or sanction-from-below, but the two are mutually exclusive. This was the either/or proposition of the middle of our century.

The fact, however, that false and true were in direct conflict and that a choice had to be made was concealed from sight because of the role played—all unknowingly, of course—by President Eisenhower. That role was the deceptive one of making many people feel, usually without articulating it, that some kind of compromise *was* possible, some kind of union or blend of genuine and spurious, not too satisfactory, perhaps, but still a blend, a bringing-together, a *modus vivendi*.

No one can think about today's ethics for very long without wondering why so much laudatory nonsense was talked about Dwight Eisenhower.

It is easy enough to see why the mass audience liked Eisenhower. Some commentators said that he was a father image to the voters with whom he was so popular, but a father is protective, custodial. A father leads onward, educates. Eisenhower was not a father image, but a mirror image to the mass audience. It was themselves they saw in "Ike"—their own unwillingness to make enemies, their own cheerful superficiality, their own vanity, their own limitations. The fact that he was a war hero gave the mass audience a moral excuse for identifying with him and seemed to put their enthusiasm on a much higher plane. It was not, however, his competence, but the fact that he was *not* competent that was the real base of his popularity. For the mass audience, Eisenhower represented an enlarged self in a position of high office.

That much is not mystifying.

But why did two such commentators as Walter Lippmann and James C. Reston come out twice against the Adlai Stevenson of '52 and '56 and then end up endorsing a John Kennedy?

Why did veteran political journalists and seasoned, sophisticated observers of the social scene keep calling Eisenhower "good"? Why didn't they ask themselves, " 'Good' in terms of what?"—" 'Good' in relation to whom?"

Columnists, magazine writers and intellectuals, though they often poked fun at the Presidential syntax, nevertheless described Eisenhower so often as "a man of good will" that it got to sound like the doxology. You wondered why they didn't sing it. Yet Eisenhower was neither a man of good will nor a man of bad will, but a man of no will.

He allowed Little Rock to develop to the point where it was a grotesquerie. He stood by and did nothing while McCarthy turned the United States Senate into a slaughterhouse. He was content to leave foreign policy to "the greatest Secretary of State America ever had," which was his description of the Prim Reaper who invented brinkmanship. He was inert and uninflected—a piece of chewing gum rolling around in the jaws of history. Nevertheless, even at the very end of his Administration, when the Washington correspondents were entirely disillusioned, they prefaced all their strictures by referring to his "decency," his "morality," his "good intentions," his "simple virtues," and his "obvious good will."

For this seemingly compulsive vocabulary, an explanation can be found, although of course it is only an hypothesis.

When a "special ethos" like that of business begins

to expand and take over the whole society, the more sensitive citizens are naturally enough aware that a change is taking place. More cutting corners goes on than formerly. More bad conduct is forgiven. Laxness mounts. There is a visible decline of moral standards. In this situation Eisenhower filled a special role. He was reiteratively called "good" and "a man of good will" in the unformulated hope that he would in some way act as a bridge between the old and the new. That is to say, through him the centuries-old idea of respect for the individual could be attached to the brand new phenomenon of the mass audience and mass popularity, so that sanction-from-below, which had come in with television and the nation-wide market, could still keep a handhold on the older, traditional ethic. To be sure, the traditional ethic would survive only in attenuated form, but (the hope was) it would survive.

Of course, it did not.

Ironically enough, the attempt to hang on to a saving remnant of the Judeo-Christian ethic by insisting on the "goodness" of Eisenhower only encouraged the growth of the pseudo-ethic. It appeared to give the masses of Eisenhower admirers more justification for their narcissistic feelings about him and it ensconced Eisenhower himself even more firmly in a position where hardly anyone dared to speak the truth about his irresponsible, indolent handling of the cares of high office.

He should not, of course, be denied whatever credit is his due. He went to Korea, and he may possibly have shortened the war by his appearance there. If he did not consciously consolidate the gains and reforms of the New Deal, he at least put no obstacles in the way of that consolidation. He had a genuine devotion to world peace where it did not involve his doing too much homework. And he certainly surprised and delighted the peace-lovers by his warning, as he left office, of the dangers inherent in the military-industrial combine.

But with the destruction of the Judeo-Christian ethic, we have lost an invaluable heritage; and if the heritage is to be recaptured, one of the first things on the agenda will have to be re-evaluating Dwight Eisenhower so that he is seen for what he really was, a moral booby trap.

It was the press, more conspicuously than any other group, who fell into the booby trap. Ever since 1952, almost all the political writing in America has been characterized by a desperate attempt to find some way of linking up the older, traditional ethic with the pseudo-ethic. The effort is still going on. After eight years of calling Eisenhower "good," the political journalists continued the hopeless cause by calling Kennedy "liberal," although Kennedy wears liberalism like nail polish. Whenever the newsmen have believed it necessary to support some government policy which was on the shabby side, they (all but a few) talked about being "realistic." Nevertheless, they failed to grasp, and they have continued in failing to grasp, a reality that dwarfs and overshadows all questions of policy.

The journalists were not the only ones who thought that Eisenhower showed how the traditional ethic and the false ethic could be made to coexist. Among certain groups of intellectuals it is currently fashionable to endorse the ex-President, rather patronizingly, by saying that an incompetent President is not always a bad thing to have, and that Eisenhower's inertness resulted in a helpful relaxation of tensions between the United States and Russia. But this assertion is based on the premise that life has periods of standing still, which it never does. However uneventful the surface, underneath things are always either progressing or retrogressing.

If we somehow bumble through without the bombs dropping, and there are historians of the future to look back on the Eisenhower Administration, it may be that the one item they will associate with it (in the perspective they will have which we do not) is the tragic thing Eisenhower did to the South by his indifference to integration.

There has long been a white liberal element in the South which wanted that region to grow up and grow out of its customs and practices about race. Way back in the 1920's there was a Southern Women's League for the Prevention of Lynching; and more recently Jonathan Daniels, author of *A Southerner Discovers the South*, observed that "the strong will for justice to the Negro [has] never been absent from the Southern scene." From the writings of such people as Lillian Smith, Mark Ethridge, P. D. East, Harry Golden, Ralph McGill, Hodding Carter and others it may fairly be concluded that a President resolved to push integration, after the Supreme Court decision was handed down, could have counted on significant cooperation from whites within the South itself.

But Presidential support was indispensable. The white liberals living in the South had to be able to say, when they approached their town councils, selectmen, vestrymen, library trustees and boards of education, "We must desegregate. The President wants it." Presidential prestige and Presidential directives were indispensable in order to remove the taint of crackpotism from whites working for equality in local situations. Presidential leadership, however, was totally lacking; and the white South, like a juvenile delinquent in a slum, was left to come of age as best it could, with violence, bitterness and waste.

What makes the situation even sadder is that the circumstances did not require Eisenhower to be a great man or a leader of heroic proportions. The situation had already developed beyond the need for that. He himself was personally popular and his office carried prestige. All he needed to have done was to have been moderately active.

In foreign affairs, Kennedy's predecessor was lazy and he was lucky. Save for the quickly surmounted U-2 crisis, nothing happened between the United

States and Russia while he was President. But within two years of his leaving office, we came to the brink of nuclear war over Cuba. On the domestic front, the relaxation induced by the incompetent President turned out to be the sort of thalidomide sedation which ultimately produced monster births like Mississippi's treatment of James Meredith. Uneventfulness—an apparent "relaxation of tensions"—in itself means nothing, one way or the other. The important question is, what kind of tides are moving underneath the seemingly motionless surface? Are they regenerative or degenerative?

Dwight Eisenhower was one of the great implanters of the pseudo-ethic, but to say that he was not "good" in terms of the older, traditional ethic is not *ipso facto* to suggest that he was *bad*. Not, at least, in the Senator Bilbo or Genghis Khan sense. He did not have horns and a tail.

The opposite of "good" in our polarized Western thinking is "bad," but there are other ways of looking at the phenomenon of Eisenhower. Eisenhower's value to the burgeoning pseudo-ethic was exactly that he really was nice, outgoing, genial—all the affirmative adjectives—but he was all these things in a way which was empty of human ethical meaning.

It was as if a friendly, grinning collie stood on the steps of the White House for eight years, waving his plumy tail at all comers, including the burglars. If you were flat on your back on the sidewalk, the collie would give you a reassuring lick in the face as he pranced on up the street to rub noses with the nearest French poodle. The book-burning speech at Dartmouth was one such amiable swipe. But the household pet is incapable of caring whether you are on the sidewalk because you are drunk, starving to death or merely eccentrically fond of stretching out on paving stones.

"How much was that doggie in the window?"

The collie's toenails made a cheerful clicking sound on the hardwood floors of the White House, but outside, the Judeo-Christian ethic was being inexorably crowded out of existence by the new pseudo-ethic and a smell was going up over the land which was not offensive to canine nostrils, but which was most distressing to human ones. It was the smell of rotting conscience.

V

An Outside Insight

WHEN MARTIN DIES first started security investigations a quarter of a century ago, it seemed like just a small racket promoted by a Texas Congressman. No one then dreamed that the security issue would later reach such proportions that to this day, in retrospect, the goings-on still seem unbelievable.

Even for those who lived through it, it is sometimes hard to realize, now, that massed superdreadnoughts took out after Annie Lee Moss and Major Peress. In 1962, Owen Lattimore published a book on his specialty, Mongolia, which was received with attention and respect; and it made one blink, seeing the reviews, to recollect that Lattimore was at one time under indictment on seven counts of perjury and that Senator McCarthy's statement that he was "the top Soviet espionage agent in the United States" was carried in headlines all across the country.

However, despite the headlines, the hysteria and the incredible accusations, there were some observers who, all through that insane period, took an ironic view. These observers saw the Communists-in-government issue as politically motivated, with the Hiss, Remington and Lattimore prosecutions basically sparked by the wish to discredit Franklin Roosevelt and the New Deal. They saw the McCarthy accusations as a new low in political brutality aimed at the same target. And certainly the presence of Richard Nixon justified the feeling some people had that the whole outcry about conspiracy, loyalty and internal subversion, deafening though it was, came down essentially to a matter of politics.

But the late George Macaulay Trevelyan once shrewdly remarked that politics is the outcome, not the cause of social change, and since Professor Trevelyan was a Tory historian and not a Marxist, the observation may be taken to be unprejudiced. If Trevelyan was correct, how does this principle apply to the Communist hysteria which gripped the United States for so long?

What was the pre-political or sub-political basis of the political paroxysm by which, alone among the Western nations, we were convulsed? Other nations had security problems, too, but those problems did not evoke a similar disturbance.

Was there an underlying social impulse peculiar to

us that heaved Whittaker Chambers and the late Senator McCarthy out of obscurity and made them headliners for so long a time?

Because of a political turmoil of the late forties and early fifties, we Americans are currently going around with a moral albatross of Chambers-Nixon plumage pendant from our necks. Is it possible that, if we asked the right questions—questions going deeper than the merely political—that unbeauteous lavaliere would drop away?

In 1950, David Riesman published a book whose very title, *The Lonely Crowd*, contained a hint that the United States had gone through a major social change. Riesman has since become a more or less ordained defender of Things-As-They-Are, and now writes from well within the Establishment. Nevertheless, many people who live outside the culture continue to feel grateful for the originality of *The Lonely Crowd* and for the sociologist's illuminating concepts of inner-directed and other-directed.

Riesman was the first to make clear to the general book-reading public that by the end of World War II, the United States was no longer a producing society but had become something quite different, namely, a consuming society. The problems of production had been solved, the solutions accelerated, no doubt, by the stimulus of war. And when hostilities were over, and the armed forces were no longer gobbling up the output of the factories, America was faced with the

new peace-time problem of how to consume the tor-
rential output of its machines. (Unlike some of its
allies, the United States did not have a ravaged land
to rebuild or a labor force decimated by millions of
casualties, military and civilian.)

The problem of consuming all the goods had to be
met within a framework where "government interference" with business (save for a few bagatelles like
tariffs and air line subsidies) had long been anathema,
and where the public had been thoroughly indoc-
trinated with the idea that any kind of controlled
economy was in the highest degree undesirable. In
Western Europe the various economic systems are a
mixture of publicly owned and privately owned enter-
prise, and are so acknowledged. In the countries of
Western Europe, the governments run the railroads.
In most of them they run the tobacco industry. In
France, the government produces Renault cars; in
Italy, Fiats. Public ownership and operation of some
parts of the industrial system is a commonplace in
Europe.

In the United States, it is different. Americans as a
nation have an hysterical blindness on the subject of
social planning. Thus when Riesman said in *The
Lonely Crowd* that consuming was the new frontier,
he was describing a situation in which (1) there was
a glut of products and (2) there was a "free enter-
prise" economy which could not be tampered with.

The only thing left that could be manipulated was
the people themselves.

These people, these Americans, had been trained in their childhood to respect the old-fashioned ideals of thrift, industry, independence and self-reliance. In addition, they had just been through four years of war during which they had all, soldiers and civilians alike, been urged to be serious and self-denying and to make sacrifices for the sake of victory over the enemy. However, if this same population was going to blot up the products which, once the war was over, poured as from a huge cornucopia out of American factories, the people would have to be changed. They would have to learn to be quite different from what they had been asked to be in wartime, and in their early training. They would have to become frivolous, self-indulgent, hedonistic and acquisitive.

In short, nothing less than their moral attitudes would have to be altered.

And since their moral attitudes came to them essentially as part of the traditional Judeo-Christian ethic, some way would have to be found to cut the ties that bound them to that ethic, so that they would drift loose and free of it.

To be sure, only some kind of omniscient deity could have seen this at the time. The unconscious direction a society takes, the social psychology it develops in response to changing conditions, does not usually become apparent except with the passage of years.

It did not take much time, however, for social scientists and other observers to note that the consuming which quickly came to dominate every aspect of post-war life was meretricious. Mankind has been consuming goods and services for thousands of years, and cannot live without doing so. But the buying and acquiring and using up which the postwar Americans learned to do (under pile-driver pressure from the advertisers) went far beyond the needs of protoplasm.

Erich Fromm, in his book *The Sane Society*, summed up succinctly the difference between normal and obsessive consumption. He described normal consuming thus:

"The act of consumption should be a concrete human act, in which our sense, bodily needs, our aesthetic taste—that is to say, in which *we* as concrete, sensing, feeling, judging human beings—are involved; the act of consumption should be a meaningful, human, productive experience."

Fromm then went on to point out that in the new consuming society, people consumed slogans, labels, "status," fantasies and fictions—the "healthy" toothpaste, "the pause that refreshes."

He concluded:

"Our way of consumption necessarily results in the fact that we are never satisfied, since it is not our real concrete person which consumes a real and concrete thing."

Thus it seems clear—from the perspective of the 1960's, at any rate—that two irreconcilable social dynamisms were at work in the postwar United States. One was a long-established ethic whose vital core is respect for the individual and which therefore has no quarrel with "good" consuming. The other was an inflexible, unadaptable economy indifferent to the individual and geared to a mass market which, in the absence of regulation, depends for survival on "bad" consuming.

No one can establish with documentation and statistics exactly how much sway the older, traditional ethic had in the United States at the end of World War II. The extent to which, at that moment in our history, the ethic molded people's judgments and opinions—how far it inspired or modified their actions —can only be a matter for surmise. But it seems possible to argue that the Judeo-Christian ethic, even fifteen or twenty years ago, was still influencing American life in two important ways.

For one thing, it kept the idea of self-discipline before people's minds as an admirable quality.

The Old Testament gives us a stern picture of Abraham preparing to sacrifice his son Isaac at the behest of God, and early Christian history is notable for the martyrs who laid down their lives for their religious beliefs. As time passed, these extremely taxing ideals of renunciation lost their force; but even the Reformation, when the ethic in effect accommodated to acquisitiveness and materialism, held up the idea of thrift and industry. Postwar America did not by any means lie all open and Danaë-like to the advertising man with his Johnny-One-Note counsel of self-indulgence:

"Fly now, pay later."

"For only pennies a day . . ."

"You can't afford *not* to own our elasticized cemetery plot."

There was a second way in which the Judeo-Christian ethic influenced postwar America—as indeed it influenced prewar America and various other Americas back through our history. The concept of respect for the individual stimulated a small but influential group of people to what might be called ethical activism. The people in this group were intellectually and morally energetic. They insisted on standards being upheld. They were *interested* in standards—and in justice, truth and fair play. The social importance of this group was once expressed by a writer in *The New Republic* who, reviewing Michael Straight's *A Very Small Remnant*, noted that "the moral salvation of the many may, and perhaps always does, depend upon the decency and courage of a very few." If national morality is high, it is usually because a comparatively small number of people (comparatively small, that is, in relation to the total population) is taking the ethic seriously.

The cultural pressures of recent years (nation-wide advertising and mass circulation magazines) have developed the genre of American "consumer" that is now so familiar. The consumer is passive; and the central drama of his life is buying. He responds to people shallowly, obediently reacting to "images" of politician or television star; depending on the neighbors to give him self-esteem by admiring his camera or his car; and relating to wife and children largely through shared experiences of acquisition.

In marked contrast to this amoeba-like character was the little phalanx of moral activists which flourished before the emergence of the pseudo-ethic and which was very much the product of the older, traditional ethic. It is hard to know what to call this company of people, particularly since the genuine examples of the type are now in eclipse and without influence. They, or various segments of them, have had an assortment of names—eggheads, reformers, New Dealers, radicals, left-wingers, bleeding hearts, liberals, intellectuals, do-gooders, Christers, Commsymps, Utopians, nigger-lovers, idealists, crusaders, agitators, etcetera. Some of the names have been admiring, some not, but the characteristic of the group was that the people in it were inner-directed. They operated, before the burgeoning of the pseudo-ethic, to provide a sort of middle-class moral leadership for the country at large.*

Some of them have been called Communist, but the important thing about them is not their politics, but their ethics. The question of whether there were Communists or former Communists in the group is irrele-

---

* To many, "middle-class" connotes greed and hypocrisy, and from Balzac to Babbitt, the record seems to back them up. But morality is a middle-class invention. The phrase is used here to suggest the standard of rectitude of men like Henry Stimson, David Lilienthal, Justice Holmes, Alexander Meiklejohn, Bishop Oxnam, Elmer Davis, Thomas L. Stokes.

vant, for where these people had made Communist commitments, they had made them for reasons of conscience—they were looking for the political philosophy which came closest to the ideal of social justice. When they found that Communism, unlike the Judeo-Christian ethic, regards some individuals as expendable, they withdrew from it.

Ethically, all these people were the leaven in the lump—the teaspoon of yeast that gives the whole long loaf its palatableness and texture.

This group, in the years directly after World War II, was far from being homogenized or from having a uniformity of membership. Though it seemed, taken as a whole, to provide a middle class moral leadership for the population as a whole, it contained within its ranks people who were not middle class—people from old families like Francis Biddle and Averell Harriman, for instance, and millionaires like Henry Wallace and Marshall Field.

Mostly it contained, however, teachers, ministers, government employees, self-employed artists, and others who lived at one remove from the industrial society. It contained any number of people from minority groups. (One of the frequently voiced complaints on the frontiers of freedom in the forties was that the Jews were almost the only Caucasians, except Eleanor Roosevelt, who would do anything about equality for Negroes, which seemed to certain other Caucasians all the more reason for blocking Negro advancement.)

The congregation of the conscientious, twenty years ago, included pacifists, philanthropists, union organizers, well-to-do graduates of the Ethical Culture School and churchmouse-poor members of the Fellowship of Reconciliation. These latter, the members of the Fellowship of Reconciliation, bravely challenged Jim Crow on Southern buses, and got thrown off and tossed into jail, a good two decades before the Freedom Riders who were their spiritual offspring. Both militant Negroes and Negroes who were described by other Negroes as Uncle Toms were part of the group, which also comprised many people who had agonized over Loyalist Spain and were never the same after Barcelona fell. Wendell Willkie was dead by the end of World War II, but he was certainly a typical member.

The phalanx included individuals who in pursuit of their ideals erred in the direction of headlong impracticality; and it contained others whose pharisaical, upper middle-class complacence about their own virtue was hard to take. There was the usual number of phonies and posturers and there was a handful of downright saints. One does not realize how puréed and featureless American character has become, under the influence of the Organization, until one looks back at the ragged conglomerate of tastes, temperaments, backgrounds and motivations which made up American moral leadership before the growth of the pseudoethic.

There are several points of significance about this

group, the first being that although it existed on sufferance in the midst of a population which overwhelmed it numerically, the people who comprised it nevertheless helped in a very substantial way to keep the general public aware of the Judeo-Christian ethic. So long as these principled people kept putting, or trying to put, their principles into practice, the ethical note of self-discipline and responsibility could not be wholly drowned out and the ethical premise of respect for the individual could not be completely overlaid and forgotten.

A second significant point about this moral leadership was that the people who comprised it were well informed. They were readers of books and assiduous readers, as a rule, of the more responsible newspapers. Hence journalistic events which were treated with much prominence and at great length, like the Hiss and Remington trials and the Oppenheimer affair, would make a deeper impression on this particular stratum of citizens than they would on casual readers and on the country in general.

A third important point about the group is that, despite the now-unfamiliar diversity of its membership, it was unified by the same feeling about social injustice that evoked the eloquence of the Judeo-Christian prophets. These were people who felt a degree of responsibility, greater or lesser, for the wetbacks, the Okies, the starving millions in India and the Negro sharecroppers at home. (It is another example of the crazy invertedness of the false ethic that today in the United States this kind of humanitarianism is almost automatically taken as a sign of "Communism.")

The most important and significant point, however, about this moral leadership of twenty years back is that, other things being equal, this group would instinctively have resisted and fought against the lowering of moral standards that became necessary when the new consuming society succeeded the producing society.

That point is of cardinal importance.

Whatever their faults—for example, all moral leadership is earnest and therefore open to the charge of humorlessness—these people were accustomed in their diversified ways to putting out, morally and intellectually. Unless they were tricked or trapped or in some way backed into it, they could not possibly have accepted the narrowness of the present-day consumer's life, with its tiny dramas of buying and acquisition, its perpetual playing-safe, its dull self-absorption and its fingernail-size horizons.

Even more important, these inner-directeds could not have stood by unprotesting while an awed subservience to popularity and "the nation-wide audience" moved in and obliterated worthier criteria.

Thus the basic situation, after peace brought its dubious blessings, was stark. The older, traditional ethic and the middle-class moral leadership which gave it actuality and tangibility were irremediably out of step with the new socio-economic development.

Something had to give.

What gave, of course, was the ethic, as the deterio-rated morals of the 1960's clearly show, and the anatomy of that defeat is the principal subject of this speculation.

Nobody openly scuttles a long-established ethic, no matter how pressing the economic need. For several reasons, a disguise must be found. In the first place, the general public, though it may honor the ethic in the breach rather than the observance, would never tolerate an undisguised attempt to get rid of it.

In the second place, an ethic is intangible, being only a set of notions in people's minds. Notions more firmly fixed in some minds than in others. It is there-fore *people* who have to be gotten rid of—who have to be silenced, discredited, immobilized and rendered ineffective—when ethic and economic structure have become irreconcilable and the ethic is under attack. Given the particular people comprising American moral leadership, a way had to be found to silence them that would keep them from fighting back, for they were accustomed to fighting for "good causes," and had the issue been clearly defined, they would have fought and might have won. Some disguise had to be found, therefore, so completely effective that the moralists would come pretty close to concurring in their own destruction.

Such a disguise *was* found, and certainly no one could have penetrated it in the confusion and insanity of the time. The witch-hunting, the treason trials, the Congressional investigations and the Communists-in-government issue provided a wonderfully noisy, effective and distracting diversion. Under cover of the diversion, the traditional ethic could be quietly dismembered and the people who implemented it branded, to their own helpless surprise, as traitors, conspirators, dupes and Communist-fronters, whose "records" would be held against them ten or even fifteen years later. Since these people were usually inveterate newspaper readers, and the newspapers were a major factor in the attack on them, the quarry was all the more confused and immobilized.

The apparent aim of the attack was to root out subversive character from entertainment, education, government, labor, industry, the military.

The real if unconscious aim was to root out character altogether in order to create faceless, automatic consumers.

And even the most detached and ironic observers, who were not for a minute taken in by the sphincter patriotism of the informers, believed the whole uproar to be political.

The foregoing is of course only a theory, a kind of post-Impressionist version of contemporary social science. Nevertheless, as a theory it may suggest an answer to the interesting question of why it was only in America, and not in other, similar Western countries like Canada and England, that we had a Whittaker Chambers, a Hiss case and the protracted epilepsy of McCarthyism.

By contrast, for instance:

In Canada, which was the center of the Soviet espionage network in North America and where the facts about the use of domestic Communists were most clearly established, the government from the very outset carefully refrained from turning the espionage problem into a grave national crisis demanding the sacrifice of traditional liberties. This is indicated by a passage in the report of the Royal Commission investigation of the Gouzenko revelations which even declines to publicize the names of those Communists, members of secret Communist cells in the government and elsewhere, who were not implicated in the espionage network. In Canada the hunt for spies has not been turned into a hunt for Communists.*

The contrast with the United States is not a flattering one, but perhaps the difference did not come about through the Canadians being nobler than we, but for the more mundane reason that the United States, at the end of World War II, was farther along the road to the mass society; the cornucopia was bigger; and the need more imperious to change the public morally, so that it would forget about self-discipline and concentrate instead, with complete self-indulgence, on buying, using up, throwing away and buying again.

Objections are sure to be raised against the idea that the seemingly political events of the treason trials and

* Benjamin Ginzburg, *Rededication to Freedom* (1959).

the Communist hunting were really socio-economic in origin. Nevertheless, in one way or another, the socio-economic is usually a factor in human affairs. For instance, it is not taking anything away from Negro Americans, in their courageous march toward full equality, to say that the expanded use of machinery had something to do with improvements in their status after World War II. As machines came more and more to do, in home and industry, what had formerly been done by a menialized Negro class, whites had less reason to resist the Negro thrust toward equality. Conversely, as Negroes were somewhat freed from soul-destroying drudgery, they had more energy to fight for their rights. (Ironically, now, in 1963, we see automation reversing the process.)

However, the Communist-infiltration fever was so melodramatic and so highly charged emotionally that many people will scoff at the suggestion that it had a socio-economic cause. Such people will be quick to make three points.

First, they will say, granted that Trevelyan was right and that politics is the outcome, not the cause of social change, was there really a social change involved? Whether as a consuming society now, or a producing society some decades ago, the United States has always been acquisitive and oriented toward possessions, and hence has always been somewhat embarrassed by the Judeo-Christian ethic. What is new about that?

Secondly, the skeptics will say, it is all very well to

talk about cutting the population loose from the older, traditional ethic, but what actual human beings performed the job? Who would consciously and deliberately set out on that kind of wrecking operation?

And thirdly, they will say, assume (for the sake of argument) that there actually were people so basely motivated that they would wipe out a nation's moral standards for the sake of securing an expanding market. How would such people go about it?

To the first question—Did a social change really occur?—it is possible to answer yes.

While the American economy was still intent upon creating its industrial system—building factories, installing machinery, improving transportation—rather than upon getting the products consumed which the system turned out, it was possible for the economy and the traditional ethic to coexist in an uneasy sort of way. There were two reasons why this coexistence was possible.

Between the virtues promoted by the economy and those called for by the ethic, there was a rough parallel. Both institutions enjoined people to be sober, responsible, self-disciplined and industrious. The economy told them to save for a rainy day. The ethic, in the innocent decades of the century, told them to forego the pleasures of earth and think of the pleasures of life everlasting. In each case, the principle of deferred pleasure was a key point.

But more importantly, the ethic, even after Darwin

and Freud and the withering-away of theology, still affirmed the importance of respect for the individual; and the economy needed self-respecting individuals (independent, self-reliant, creative) while it was still concerned with the problems of production.

A second reason why ethic and economy could somehow manage to hobble along together was that, in the producing economy, there was a margin for maneuver. The arts, religion, agriculture, the academic world and the home had not yet been drawn completely into the orbit of commercialization. During the years when the United States was engaged in building up its industrial system, there were still places you could live or occupations you could follow which were at one remove from industrial production.

And therein lies the social change whose ultimate outcome was the political phenomenon of Congressional investigations, loyalty programs and so on. The producing society did not require *everyone* to be a producer, and the people (like housewives) who were not producing could act as a sort of brake on the people who were. The consuming society, on the other hand, overwhelmed with goods and commodities, can make no exceptions. *In the consuming society, everyone has to consume.* The margin for maneuver is abolished; the brakes are off.

The second question critics will raise is, What actual human beings could or would seek to destroy the older, traditional ethic?

The prompt answer must be that no conscious villainy was involved. Nobody *wanted* to get rid of the Judeo-Christian ethic. The late William Remington, when struggling against double jeopardy, entrapment and other things that are not supposed to happen to Americans, once remarked to a reporter, "All through history, there have always been people who got in the way."

A society had sharply changed its direction, and there were people who got in the way.

Other people got them out of the way, and these other people certainly regarded themselves as political instruments. Richard Nixon, for instance.

The agencies which got them out of the way appeared to be merely political. The China Lobby. The House Un-American Activities Committee. The Senate Internal Security Sub-Committee. The politically passionate American Legion. The Republican-oriented press, which printed in banner headlines every single accusation made by Senator McCarthy.

Some of the people who destroyed the older, traditional ethic and the middle-class moral leadership which carried it on sincerely believed that by "opposing Communism" they were being virtuous. Others, more cynically, knew themselves to be engaged in power politics. But even the cynics, opportunistically creating for their own aggrandizement a climate of fear and hysteria, had no idea they were doing anything that went beyond political maneuver.

It all happened so fast. Elected in the Republican landslide of 1946, Senator McCarthy was just another member of the Senate. . . . Then, in 1950, as the time for his reelection campaign approached, he sought an issue and found it. He made a speech accusing the State Department of harboring 205 (or 81 or 57; the number he used is disputed) Communists on its staff. To his own surprise, *and for reasons that have never been sufficiently explained,* a few newspapers played up the speech.*

It often happens that human beings do things whose roots go far deeper than the performers themselves are aware. As Shaw pointed out in *Saint Joan,* the people of fifteenth-century Europe had no idea that feudalism was on the way out and nationalism was arising to take its place. Nevertheless, they did things, like crowning the Dauphin at Rheims, which promoted the growth of nation-states. Similarly, nobody in America in the late forties realized, or could have realized, that a glut of products, combined with a sacred, untouchable, sarcophagus-economy, was going to necessitate a lowering of moral standards. Things were done, however, which, though they were quite on the unconscious level, effectively dragged the standards down.

The third question sure to be asked is: How does anyone get rid of an ethic? Particularly one so long established as that which has descended to us from our Jewish and Christian forebears?

* Italics mine. Anthony Lewis, Pulitzer Prize-winning reporter, reviewing Richard H. Rovere's *Senator Joe McCarthy,* *New York Times,* June 21, 1959.

One thing you do *not* do. You do not tell people that the rules have now been changed, and urge them to go out and be naughty and do evil and flout all the precepts they learned at their mothers' knees.

The only possible way to get rid of an ethic is to substitute another ethic. Or rather, what *appears* to be another ethic. And that, oddly enough, is where Whittaker Chambers comes in. If there was any one turning point in the change-over from producing to consuming as "our way of life," the symbolic figure of Whittaker Chambers marks it. To be sure, there were scores of little Chamberses who went into the witnessing business. There were enough of them to create the density of atmosphere we call a climate. But Chambers was the prototype.

The Hiss case was not an isolated occurrence, though some people think of it as such. It was part of a sociological progression. The *New Yorker* writer A. J. Liebling emphasized this point in the chapter on the Hiss case in his book *The Press*. The metropolitan newspapers, Liebling said, by their abuse of both the judge who presided at the first Hiss trial and the jurors who voted for acquittal, made it a psychological impossibility for a second judge and jury to find the defendant anything but guilty. A guilty verdict was doubly guaranteed, according to Liebling, by the refusal of the United States District Court to grant Hiss a change of venue.

Liebling concluded as follows:

The true beneficiary of the newspaper jury tampering was Senator Joseph McCarthy of Wisconsin, who for four years had been hovering above the battle, waiting for somebody to drop safely dead before he swooped. The conviction of a fairly high former official, a Democrat, like Hiss, gave McCarthy his cue, and a couple of weeks after the end of the second trial, he made his famous first West Virginia speech, in which he announced there were hundreds of card-carrying Communists in the State Department. When anybody muttered that he could not prove his charges, he would shake his necrophagous beak and croak: "Who would have believed it of Alger Hiss?"

The stultification of justice in the Hiss trial by the press had given the fearless statesman from Wisconsin courage to be born.

Chambers, brought into the floodlights by the Hiss case, was one of the first significant symbols of the pseudo-ethic. He personified anti-Communism, a cardinal virtue of the new pseudo-ethic, and the hidden message conveyed by his appearance on the social scene, and by the endorsements he received, was none the less effective for being subliminal.

The message was that all the sins and faults of which Chambers might have been thought guilty, if he were judged in terms of the old ethic, were now outweighed and transcended. The transgressions were redeemed and Chambers was made pure by this new virtue, anti-Communism. And this new virtue had become much more important (after all, your country is in peril, isn't it?) than anything we formerly thought of as good behavior.

During the Communists-in-government turmoil, many troubled newspaper readers thought wistfully that everything would be so much easier if only Whittaker Chambers were a more admirable man. But it was precisely the fact that he was *not* admirable that made him the harbinger of the new pseudo-ethic.

There have been other famous American trials—Tom Mooney, Sacco and Vanzetti—but who remembers the witnesses? All three cases—Mooney, Sacco and Vanzetti, Hiss—were alike in being, not so much trials, as acted-out object lessons. The pursuit of justice on each occasion was something less than sedulous. But there was an extra dimension to the Hiss case which the others did not have.

The Mooney and Sacco and Vanzetti cases were, sociologically speaking, exactly what they appeared to be. They were exercises in tossing somebody out. But the Hiss case, though it appeared on the surface to be concerned only with getting rid of Hiss—despite his strenuous objections—had a subtle, hidden dynamic. That dynamic was not only to get the defendant *out*, but—what many people would have objected to, if it had appeared to them without disguise—to get Chambers *in*. Innumerable commentators have referred to Alger Hiss as "enigmatic," but it was not the defendant who was enigmatic. It was the case itself.

VI

The Possibility of Change

Thus far this speculation has been concerned with insight and understanding.

But what about action?

People need to realize what has been going on. Their minds need to be opened to the possibility of change.

Is there any kind of public action of the sort usually taken by "leaders" that can help to bring this about? And is there anything personal the individual can do by himself? On this score, a few more things may be said.

A more vigorous morality will require bringing back into American life that moral leadership which was silenced and immobilized in the turmoil of the late forties and early fifties. However, this segment of the population—now mostly middle-aged or older, of course—cannot again begin to give expression to the Judeo-Christian ethic until the pseudo-ethic is first disestablished. The pseudo-ethic came in with symbols, and if it goes out, it will have to go out the same way. This is why, although it seems odd to talk about a detective story in connection with morality and ethics, further reference must be made to the Hiss case.

Most of the prominent figures who embodied the false ethic are now so welded into the culture as to be un-get-at-able. Their sins are taken for granted as part of the natural order of things and they have faded into the landscape. But there is one pillar of the pseudo-ethic whose plaster sainthood might be demolished and that is Whittaker Chambers. What makes this conceivable, even though Chambers is dead, is the recurrent suggestion (it came up again upon the publication, in 1962, of Richard Nixon's *Six Crises*) that Hiss might have been framed.

A lobster grows another claw when he loses one in a fight, and perhaps many people assume, tacitly, that America will eventually replace its traditional ethic in the same way. After a period of some discomfort, a new generation will come along—a generation that is vague about Hiss and that never heard of Remington and Lattimore. These young people, born late enough to have escaped direct experience of Senator McCarthy's career, will somehow make a fresh start and get us back on the right track.

It is a nice idea, but unworkable.

". . . contrary to some people's opinion," says Bruno Bettelheim, "youth does not create its own cause for which it is ready to fight. All it can do is to embrace causes developed by mature men." *

The pseudo-ethic cannot simply be left to the eroding passage of time, because as long as Chambers' reputation with the general public is one of purity and patriotism, the mechanism of intimidation is still intact. This mechanism is not being used as much as it was a few years ago. That is no longer necessary. But it has never been dismantled and it could be revived again at a moment's notice.

The mere existence of the mechanism of intimidation means, politically, that the extreme Right can influence government policy to an extent completely out of proportion to the actual numbers of its followers.† Psychologically, the mechanism sits like a thirty-ton granite tombstone on top of any hope of reviving a middle-class moral leadership.

"It is pretty generally agreed," wrote Gerald Johnson in the April 16, 1962, issue of *The New Republic*,

* *Daedalus*, Winter 1962, "The Problem of Generations."

† In his syndicated column of January 18, 1963, Marquis Childs wrote: "The ingredient lacking in the political mixture, in the view of some of the Kennedy players and particularly on Capitol Hill, is conviction. There is little sense of the politics of conviction. One of the ablest and most loyal of [Kennedy's] lieutenants on the Hill put it this way:

"that it was the typewriter that sunk Hiss, and it sunk him because the jury believed—and Hiss's own counsel at the time believed—that it was authentic because there was no possible way in which the prosecution could have planted a fake. Now Nixon's book reveals that there was a way. . . ."

Chambers is anchored in our culture by the typewriter, but as long ago as April, 1952, *The Progressive* published an article by Professor Fred Rodell of the Yale Law School entitled "Was Alger Hiss Framed?" In the more than ten years since, two responsible studies have been made which focused on the possibility of forgery by typewriter in the Hiss case. One was done by Professor Herbert L. Packer, associate professor of law at Stanford University, and one by Fred J. Cook, former crime reporter for the New York *World-Telegram* and author of *The Unfinished Story of Alger Hiss* (1958).

Nevertheless, although many people have continued to be troubled, right down to the present day, by the idea of sending a man to prison on the word of

---

" 'It's true that the conviction somehow doesn't come through. But you have to say this, too. There is no opposition from the left of the center. The only active, crusading force in the political picture comes from the radical right. . . .' "

Childs goes on to say: ". . . The political landscape—if, indeed, the word *political* can be applied to it—is a bland, more or less featureless terrain. One of the few conspicuous landmarks is the shadow cast by the extreme right."

Whittaker Chambers, no spontaneous crusade was generated by intimations that the typewriter might have been faked. Perhaps the contrast seemed too extreme—an ordinary, commonplace machine and a lot of detective-story minutiae on one side, and the careers and earnest activities of a great many grown men (some of them celebrities) on the other. In terms of this essay, however, one may weigh in on the side of the typewriter the possibility that there was a deeplying sociological reason for framing Hiss.

Nixon in *Six Crises* inadvertently revealed that the FBI had had the famous Woodstock in its possession four months before Hiss's attorneys "found" it. The former Vice President quickly disclaimed his *gaffe*, but Hiss's lawyers, reviewing the record in the light of Nixon's statement, found a report of the House Un-American Activities Committee dated December 31, 1951, which read as follows:

"The committee wishes to commend the Federal Bureau of Investigation for its work in bringing this case (the Hiss case) to a successful conclusion. The location of the typewriter and certain other pieces of evidence needed during the trial of the case was amazing."

In an article in *The Nation* of May 12, 1962, entitled "The Ghost of a Typewriter," Fred J. Cook wrote:

This disclosure [the HUAC report] is the most recent and the most official in a long series, all tending in the same direction, all pointing to the same conclusion—that the

government *did* find the typewriter it vows on its honor *
it never had in its possession. The point is vital, for the
prosecution of Alger Hiss was either an honest prosecution
or it was a frame-up. There is no middle ground in this
case for an innocent mistake; for documents and a typewriter are not honestly mistaken or personally prejudiced
eyewitnesses. They are hard bits of physical evidence, and
they are either legitimate or utter and callous frauds.

In conclusion, Cook says:

Time and again too many persons in high official capacity, in full position to know, have revealed that the truth
about the finding of the typewriter is the exact reverse of
what it had to be if the government's case were a valid
case. The clear indications are that a typewriter was found
by government agents a full four months before the Hisses
captured Woodstock No. 230,099. Almost certainly, if
that is so, this machine is a fraudulent machine that was
planted on the defence.

Rodell in his article in 1952 expressed great admiration for the work of Chester Lane in preparing Hiss's
motion for a new trial. Lane opened up the possibility
of forgery by typewriter. He conceived the idea of

* When Hiss's attorney, the late Chester Lane, filed a
motion for a new trial, on the basis of evidence he had col-
lected of forgery by typewriter, the government replied with
an affidavit from Earl J. Connelley, assistant director in
charge of field operations for the FBI in the Hiss case. Connelley said under oath that the FBI "does not have in its
possession and never did have in its possession any typewriter
known, believed, or considered to be the Woodstock machine."

giving some pages typed on the Woodstock No. 230,-099 to a typewriter engineer—one Martin K. Tytell of New York—and asking him whether, without ever seeing the Woodstock, he could make another typewriter which would produce typed documents similar in peculiar typing characteristics to the samples.

Lane's experiment was seriously hampered by the fact that many people who could have helped him refused to do so, being unwilling to get involved in the Hiss case. There were also intimations that several potential witnesses had been given a strong hint by the FBI that they would do themselves no good if they tried to help Hiss. Lane furthermore had the disability of a time limit in getting the motion for a new trial before the court. Nevertheless, despite great handicaps, he did succeed in having a machine produced which two experts, who happened to know the circumstances of its manufacture, said would have fooled them if they had not been forewarned.

Professor Rodell began his piece by saying that he himself had never been "either a Hiss-lover or a Chambers-lover" and that he had always thought both men lied or at least never told the whole truth. Then he scored the press roundly for having ignored some almost fantastically "newsworthy" items in Lane's motion. After which he remarked:

But when I finished reading the motion for a new Hiss trial I was deeply shaken. Not that I was convinced of Hiss's innocence. But—assuming always the complete honesty of the lawyer who drew up the motion (and

Chester Lane is a thoroughly reputable citizen with no tags, so far as I can discover, that even Joe McCarthy could pin on him save only his courageous championing of Hiss)—I was convinced that, regardless of Hiss's innocence or guilt, his conviction was procured in large part by the use of highly suspect and very possibly manufactured evidence; I was convinced that there was something quite malodorous, to put it mildly, about certain FBI activities in connection with the case (is this perhaps why the press petered out on the story?); and I was convinced that Hiss is entitled, if not to a new trial forthwith, at least to such help from the court as his attorneys need to round up further evidence to which they have leads, but which they now have no power to procure—evidence of a sort that would make a new trial clearly mandatory.

Six years after Rodell's piece, Professor Packer wrote a paper for the May, 1958, issue of the *Stanford Law Review* entitled "A Tale of Two Typewriters." It was a summary of research done under a grant from the Fund for the Republic, the purpose of the research being "to study the testimony of former members of the Communist Party who became government witnesses in court trials, Congressional and administrative proceedings relating to the issue of Communism." Of the Hiss case, Packer wrote:

"Here is a *cause célèbre* of the first magnitude, whose political repercussions far transcend the immediate issues determined by Hiss's perjury conviction. Yet many of the facts on whose assumed existence weighty judgments of public policy have been made remain in doubt."

At the end of his paper, he remarked:

"Whatever else may be said about Mr. Lane's motion for a new trial, it has certainly raised questions which deserve more definitive answers than have yet been forthcoming."

Packer included his "Tale of Two Typewriters" in a book called *Ex-Communist Witnesses,* which he published in 1962. In his book, he concluded that despite the haunting, unresolved doubts which are still current, the Hiss case should not be reopened.

"We should do better to forego knowledge in favor of repose," wrote Packer.

"Repose" scarcely seems the word to describe the atmosphere in which we currently live, and even Packer, who concentrates on the actual technicalities of possible typewriter forgery and eschews any larger views, ends up by saying, "But it should be clear that now as we close the books on the Hiss case it must be with the consciousness that we have stopped far short of even so imperfect an approximation of 'truth' as the processes of law permit."

Packer in 1962 had no sooner finished pleading for repose than another book was published on the subject. Entitled *A Tragedy of History,* it was a collection, put together by his son, of the papers of the late Bert Andrews, *Herald Tribune* reporter who worked enthusiastically with Nixon and the House Un-American Activities Committee to get Hiss indicted. In view of this partisan background, it is interesting that Andrews should have said, in his conclusion, "It is easy to say that Alger Hiss is guilty. It is less easy to say what he is guilty of."

The possibility of fraud was once again brought up by Kingsley Martin, reviewing for the *New Statesman* (January 11, 1963) a book called *The Quiet Canadian*. The Quiet Canadian was Big Bill Donovan's Canadian opposite number, in World War II, and the book tells how this government administrator set up a workshop, under cover of the Canadian Broadcasting Company, where experts learned how to forge documents undetectably. After remarking that such "special operations" of government are often wrongly supposed to have come to an end with the war, Martin goes on to say:

"Any of us, it is clear, can lose our reputations . . . if we sufficiently annoy any government or group of persons in possession of an efficient factory of forgeries; we shall be condemned by public opinion and by a court of law. What makes the Hiss trial so profoundly unsatisfactory was that no one can be quite sure . . . whether certain damning documents were genuine or not."

The continuing vitality of the Hiss case, the unease it still arouses in many thoughtful people, is, paradoxically, reassuring. It shows that, although America seems on the surface largely committed to the pseudo-ethic, there is a saving remnant of healthy conscience and pre-Chambers morality underneath. Indeed, the very hostility which discussion of the case evokes among those who have embraced Chambers as hero and standard-bearer shows an unconscious fear that the Judeo-Christian ethic is still alive in men's memories. The hostility was much in evidence, it will be recalled, in November of 1962, when Howard K. Smith put Hiss on a television program that was described as Nixon's political obituary.

A practical issue comes up here—namely, whether there is any way in law, or any duly constituted investigative procedure, by which the bona fides of the Hiss typewriter could at this late date be explored. Packer considered the idea and made two suggestions. One (whose inherent dangers he was quick to admit) was that a carefully selected committee chosen from both houses of Congress should look into the matter. He emphasized that such a committee would have to be under the leadership of someone exceptionally intelligent, strong-fibered, upright and just; and although he did not mention Samuel Seabury, presumably he had someone of that caliber in mind.*

Packer's other suggestion was that some sort of American equivalent of the British Royal Commission be formed, made up of men and women of professional distinction and known capacity for disinterestedness.

* It is a sign of the times that one has to go back as far as Seabury for the figure of the dedicated, crusading lawyer who is known to the general public. There are still such lawyers around, but their horizons have closed in. Or perhaps one might say that Seabury's mantle descended to Perry Mason!

Of course, an Attorney General with a keen wish to resolve all doubts about fraud in the Hiss case could do much to facilitate an impartial and convincing investigation.

But the *how* is less important than the push to do it.

Apropos of the push to do it, this writer is reminded of having served many years ago, during World War II, on the Race Relations Committee of the Stage Door Canteen in Times Square, New York. World War II was fought on a segregated basis, and the Stage Door Canteen had the distinction of being one of only (so far as we knew) two canteens in the country which entertained both white and Negro servicemen on a footing of equality. We committee members were young then—young enough to have been surprised and taken aback at finding it was not only conservative people and prejudiced people who deplored the Canteen's courageous break with current practice. Some of the people whom we had taken to be liberals deplored it, too.

"That's all very well," said these liberals petulantly, when we spoke about the Canteen's no-discrimination policy, "but you haven't produced a solution."

It took a while to realize that this was only half the sentence. The rest of the sentence, left unsaid, was:

". . . and until you do, I am absolved from responsibility about Negroes."

With the passage of years, one learns how to answer the deflating remark about not having produced a solution.

The answer is that you never *start* with a solution.

The solution is what develops after you have begun working on something which apparently has no solution.

This has been true of whatever progress has been made toward racial equality; it will be true of the peace movement, if it succeeds in achieving peace; and it will also be true of the rehabilitation of the Judeo-Christian ethic.

Last year, Chief Justice Warren—alarmed, as are others, by our declining standards of morality—suggested setting up a Board of Ethics to rule on what constitutes good behavior. But Boards of Ethics do not get any messages across to the general public. The most effective message-sending we have seen recently has been done by an emergent minority. In Nashville, Little Rock, New Rochelle, Albany, Oxford, and Birmingham, the Negro community has said that it does not intend to be stopped, and has said it so clearly that even people who read nothing but the comics and the sports page have begun to get the idea.

Message-sending is an indispensable part of social change. Hence, since anti-Communism as a domestic issue is the keystone in the arch of the pseudo-ethic, one effective way to demolish that false edifice is to knock the props out from under the professional anti-Communists, beginning with the vulnerable Witness.

So much for a possible public action by "all in Civil Authority" as it says in the Book of Common Prayer.

But what about private and personal action?

Not many people, after all, are in a position themselves to do anything about the professional anti-Communists. But there is one thing that anyone can do to bring back the older, traditional ethic, and that is to use it—i.e., consistently to make judgments, and form and express opinions, on the basis of respect for the individual, rather than on the basis of what will maintain the one-institution society.

Such a course of action will, naturally, bring one into conflict with the conventional wisdom, popular opinion and Ritual Lies. There is, nevertheless, no underestimating its importance, for exposing the falsity of the pseudo-ethic is only half the job—the other half being to put the traditional ethic back into circulation.

Refusing to compromise with the pseudo-ethic and taking a flat-out stand on the older, traditional ethic is probably most important in the area of politics and recent political history, for *according to the Judeo-Christian ethic, there was nothing ethically wrong with having had Communist sympathies or Communist involvements in the thirties.* To disavow and apologize for such feelings or actions is to concede that "anti-Communism" is not only a virtue (which it is not), but that it is a more important virtue than telling the truth under oath, refusing to "name names," or wanting to help the disinherited of the earth.

Many of the people who were attacked during the treason-trial-and-McCarthy era for having once had Communist ties, either slight or intensive, apologized for those ties. Laid low by journalistic napalm about "national peril," the apologizers could not have seen what only hindsight and the subsequent deterioration of morals revealed—to wit, that in their apologies they were falsifying, without meaning to, a part of their life experience. They were treating as undignified what had often had its own dignity, even though in the event a sincerely held belief proved erroneous.*

The passage of time has showed that these disavowals are incantatory, but they continue to be published. The following is part of an article in the *Atlantic* † entitled "The Bitter '30's: From a Personal History," by Alfred Kazin, and deals with the writer's disillusionment about the Nazi-Soviet Pact a quarter of a century ago.

All my life I had lived among people who had seemed to me beautiful because they were the dust of the earth; I had taken literally the claim that they identified their

* Of course, some people were attacked for having had Communist ties who had not had them, and these gentry were in the position of having to make a clumsy-sounding avowal—i.e., "I didn't, but it would have been all right if I had." As a witty woman poet once remarked in this connection, "They try to make you feel guilty because you did too much for Loyalist Spain, whereas in your own mind you feel bad because you didn't do *enough* for Loyalist Spain."

† May, 1962.

own suffering with the liberation of humanity. I now saw that many of these people had no moral imagination whatever. They were as cold as their leader, as self-concerned, heartless, as mediocre; but being Communists, they existed by an intellectual pretension from which their stupidity could never deliver them. Day after day I followed the *Daily Worker* with savage joy at its confusion as those who had been so eloquent about the Okies, the unemployed, the victims of fascism, now tried to explain the secret contribution that the noble Stalin, the great Stalin, the all-wise and far-seeing Stalin, had made to the cause of world peace.

Morally unimaginative.
Cold.
Self-concerned.
Heartless.
Mediocre.
Intellectually pretentious.
Stupid.

It takes a minute to realize that the people thus described are Americans, rather better educated than the general run, and long-time associates of the writer's.

Granted the horrified recoil of idealists from the Hitler-Stalin Pact, the passage above is nevertheless overdramatized and fake. In his other writings, Kazin has shown himself to be perspicacious above the average, so if his friends were as bad as he says they were, it should not have required a political *détente* in Eastern Europe to make him aware of the fact. This is automated, mechanized writing—as artificial as the perpetually smiling families in television commercials.

One says "heartless," "mediocre" and "stupid" about Communists as inevitably as one says "contour," "uplift" and "cleavage" about brassieres, and with about the same net result in verisimilitude.

However, purifying litanies like the above have now become routine. They are an example of the Ritual Lie—the comfortable, neighborly, mindless cliché which reassures, as once Caucasians were reassured by agreeing happily together that Negroes are just like children and are all right in their place.

For erstwhile left-wingers, of course, some such bit of copywriting as the one quoted is the price of admission to the Establishment.

Aside from knowing how to evaluate "anti-Communism," there are other ways in which the single individual can help to re-establish the older, traditional ethic. The pseudo-ethic came into the culture largely via politics, but contemporary literature, both "intellectual" and popular, plays an important role in keeping it ascendant.

In part, this is not surprising. One expects the *Reader's Digest* type of storytelling to follow the line of the false ethic. One expects a novel like *The Man in the Gray Flannel Suit* to evade the issue of standing up to the boss. One is not surprised that *Advise and Consent* equates political enlightenment with homosexuality. But many of the prestige books and plays operate unconsciously to depress, discourage and inhibit that group of people upon whom the regeneration of the traditional ethic depends. Such books and plays have this effect because the authors mistake the part for the whole.

What is notable about the prestige dramas and novels of the present time is that so many of them are concerned with sex, drug addiction and various degraded forms of behavior. Elizabeth Hardwick, in an impressionist piece called "Grub Street: New York," * has an author of the old-fashioned kind saying, "If you're not a pederast, a junkie, a Negro—not even a 'white Negro,' ha, ha!—you haven't a dog's chance! Just put your foot in a publisher's office and someone will step on it!"

One of the excuses offered by many reviewers for the preoccupation of some intellectually fashionable writers with drugs, crime, drink and sex deviations—at the expense of a broader view of life—is that these artists are displaying "compassion." Edmund Fuller is one of the few critics who has perceived the hollowness of the claim that choice of this kind of material in itself shows compassion. In his book of essays, *Man in Modern Fiction*, he discusses a book called *Flee the Angry Strangers*, by George Mandel, in which the eighteen-year-old heroine is addicted to drugs, sexually delinquent and the mother of an illegitimate child. Fuller says:

As this girl . . . steps up the dope, takes on more men indiscriminately, and tries a little prostitution, she can still say, reproachfully, "You think I'm a tramp."

* *New York Review of Books*, February, 1963.

"Shucks, kid," is the general attitude of the new-compassion boys, "just going around doing everything a tramp does, doesn't make a good, sweet, clean, little kid like you a tramp."

In short, the new compassion is the denial that men and women are what their consistent, voluntary (and involuntary) patterns of action make them. The elements of true tragedy and compassion—the fall from a standard, responsibility however extenuated, repentance and the struggle for rehabilitation—are not in this philosophy.

There seems to be a generalized literary theory floating about that the pederast-junkie-white-Negro writers, in their concern with addiction, reflect symbolically the fact that we are all addicted to something. It seems also to be felt that in their portrayals of degraded behavior, such writers are saying with honesty and stoic courage, "This is the way things really are" (the refrain which runs through Jack Gelber's *The Connection*).

But this is blindness.

Addiction suggests helplessness, subjection, self-absorption and a concern with one's own private welfare. The plays and novels about it, though seemingly so far from "the dismal science" of economics, are really nothing more than obedient projections and romanticizations of the dazed, bargain-happy consumer in the discount house. Furthermore, the supposedly stoic refrain of "This is the way things really are," is in its essence a dutiful denial of the possibility of change.

To be sure, we are all addicted to something. *Of*

Human Bondage is a novel about addiction, but there is more to Philip Carey than his enslavement by a sleazy waitress. At the same time that he is living through his victimization by Mildred, Philip is also courageously and intelligently stepping down in a highly self-conscious class society because financial considerations make it necessary. We remember Maugham's hero as well for his unrepining, un-self-pitying fortitude during the seemingly hopeless period of his employment in the draper's shop as we do for his subjection to Mildred. Helpless as he is with Mildred, handicapped as he is by Mildred, he nevertheless takes responsibility for his education and for launching himself in his profession.

The message of resignation, the persuasion to moral irresponsibility, comes to us, in some of our contemporary literature, in disguised form; but it comes to us. Some of the most highly spoken of creative talents in this country stand hand in hand with the checker from the A & P, both artist and supermarket employee asking, with the spurious modesty of the pseudo-ethic, "Who am I to say what's right and wrong?"

This slipperiness is not good for the fellow from the A & P: for the writer it is disastrous. His real message, far from being impassive and courageous, is highly inflected, propagandistic and quite the opposite of courageous. His real message is, "This is the way things *have to be*. Rebellion is useless." Just as much as the Establishment social scientists and the writers in the liberal magazines ostensibly scolding about waste and vulgarity, the supposedly detached artist is actually preaching the doctrine of resigned acceptance of the *status quo*.

It is disastrous for a writer not to be aware of the implications of what he is saying, but the disaster does not stop there. Since, as unwitting prisoners of the pseudo-ethic, so many of these writers will make no commitments about good and evil, they can have no conflict worthy of the name. Nor can they have any characters with whom reader or playgoer instinctively identifies. Hence such authors have no way to hold an audience save by shock tactics—the rape, the brutality, the scarifying language. There is no place, however, where the law of diminishing returns sets in faster or more implacably than in the use of shock and outrage as a means of compelling attention. What the prestige writer has really done, therefore, is to cut himself off—or to permit the society to cut him off—from the chance to grow.

In Robert Bolt's play *A Man for All Seasons*, one of the characters says to Sir Thomas More, "If you must rebel, rebel in one of the places where it's been provided for." The intellectually fashionable writers, for all their violence and their seeming fury of distaste for the television society, are rebelling in the places provided.

Nothing shows so clearly that they have been tamed as their concentration on what are called "interpersonal relationships" and the absence from their works of any reference to politics or economics—i.e., to man in his social context. Edward Albee's play *Who's Afraid of Virginia Woolf?* is a case in point. This, too, is a play about addiction. The two most prominent characters are a history professor and his wife who drink steadily and quarrel bitterly from two in the morning until dawn. In all the torrent of verbiage, however, there is hardly a single reference to students, to curriculum, to faculty or, what seems strange for a history teacher, to politics.

Of course, one has no right to hand an author a list of issues and say, "Base your next play or novel on one of these." But one does have the right to demand complexity, texture, depth and a sense of the layeredness and many-sidedness of life. This the prestige writers are, for the most part, unable to convey. Tennessee Williams, certainly their dean, has gone all the way to cannibalism in his description of "interpersonal relations," * and it is perhaps significant that Elia Kazan, in the directions for staging *Streetcar*, describes Stan Kowalski as "a walking penis."

What is that, in essence, but the One-Trait Personality of the public relations boys?

In contrast to the shock tactics and the exclusions of the admired writers of our time, one thinks of the opening pages of *Anna Karenina* and Tolstoy's mischievous description of Oblonsky:

"And so liberalism had become a habit of Stepan Arkadyevitch's, and he liked his newspaper, as he did

* *One Arm, and Other Stories* (1948), "Desire and the Black Masseur."

his cigar after dinner, for the slight fog it diffused in his brain."

But it can be taken as a good sign that the prestige books and plays are not producing full-bodied satisfaction in either critics or audiences. The reviews and critiques are attentive and polite. There is, after all, little other intellectual fare save "mass entertainment." Nevertheless, a vaguely reproachful atmosphere exists of hungry sheep looking up and not being fed.

The element which is felt and sensed as missing, in these unconsciously propagandistic writers, is authority. The implicit air of command.

"Never forget," Rilke said to his wife, as he lay dying, "that life is magnificent;" and Van Wyck Brooks remarked in *The Writer in America* that the great writers are the ones who make you feel that the game is worth the candle, that life is worth living. It is the writer's job to look over the rim of the culture in which he happens to be living and speak to people of the universals which are common to all human life. If he fails to do that, he fails to acquire the one true earmark of any professional of any kind—the implicit air of command.

Every once in a while the shock tactics in highbrow and/or lowbrow literature inspire someone like David Susskind or the P.E.N. Club or the New York *Herald Tribune* to hold a forum on whether or not we ought to have censorship. The panelists at these discussions are usually unhappy. They agree, as a general thing, that we should not impose censorship, but the position is not one they can support with relish, for who wants to be the gallant, plumed and helmeted champion of a novel about transvestites?

And, of course, we do not need censorship.

We need a responsible public, even if it is quite a small one, that reacts in terms of the older, traditional ethic and rejects those writers, however highly spoken of, who are all unwittingly in the service of the pseudo-ethic.

No society is eager for its own dissolution and all societies try—instinctively, as it were—to perpetuate the *status quo*. In our times, however, the means for suggesting resignation and quashing protest are powerful, saturative and all-pervasive. But there is one way to throw off these cultural shackles, and that is to think of a situation where there *really* is no possibility of change.

Such situations exist.

The scientists have been telling us recently that we have pretty much come to the end of the road so far as exploration of sub-atomic particles is concerned. The gamma rays which are used to examine these particles so distort what is being looked at that the scientist can no longer trust the validity of what he sees.

Finally, I come to what it seems to me may well be from the long range point of view the most revolutionary of the insights to be derived from our recent experiences in physics, more revolutionary than the insights afforded by the discoveries of Galileo and Newton, or of Darwin. This is the insight that it is impossible to transcend the human reference point . . . The new insight comes from a realization that the structure of nature may eventually be such that our processes of thought do not correspond to it sufficiently to permit us to think about it at all. We have already had an intimation of this in the behavior of very small things in the quantum domain . . . there can be no difference of opinion with regard to the dilemma that now confronts us in the direction of the very small. We are now approaching a bound beyond which we are forever stopped from pushing our inquiries, not by the construction of the world, but by the construction of ourselves.*

What is true of the very small may also prove true of the very large. Doors may eventually slam in our faces in intergalactic space. Considered in this kind of perspective, the recasting of a man-made society seems to come within the limits of the possible. Another factor, too, suggests the feasibility of change. The existence of a pseudo-ethic is in a way a left-handed compliment to human beings. It reveals their deep-rooted need for moral order.

Only one question need be asked, but it is basic.

What kind of social climate would permit the existence of the Judeo-Christian ethic and of a moral leadership which—allowing for human fallibility, of course —would endeavor to carry it into operation?

* P. W. Bridgman, "Philosophical Implications of Physics," *Bulletin of the American Academy of Arts and Sciences*, February, 1950.

The answer seems to be a multi-institution society.

R. H. Tawney said a long time ago that industrialism is no more the necessary characteristic of an economically developed society than militarism is a necessary characteristic of a nation which maintains military forces.* A few years ago one used to hear a great deal in intellectual circles about "cultural pluralism," which was supposed to be a major benefit of America's melting-pot society. "Cultural pluralism" ceased to be heard of at just about the point where somebody started marketing a food product called Milady's Blintzes, but the answer to our present situation—the "solution," if one has to have that word—would seem to be *institutional* pluralism.

When Congress reconvened in January of 1963, most of the top-flight political writers pointed out that that body is now so riddled with anachronisms and so badly in need of redesigning that it has almost lost the capacity to function. However, although informed people are aware of this circumstance, nothing will be done. Nothing will be done because government is not currently one of our institutions.† As Marquis Childs says, the political landscape is a bland, more or less featureless terrain. In a multi-institution society, on the other hand, government would function as a social entity in its own right, and there would be at least a fair chance of initiating Congressional reform.

* *The Acquisitive Society* (1921).

† In the U.S.S.R., which is also a one-institution society, government is the one institution, just as business is over here.

To create a diversified, pluralistic society would, of course, mean cutting business back so that it became the equal of, rather than the superior of, education, government, the family, religion and the arts. That is to say, its claims would not be allowed to override the claims of other institutions.

This would mean planning, regulation and Grand Designs whose wellspring was respect for the individual. Vested interests would be challenged by newly articulate interests, now mute. The family, for instance, would protect its teen-agers from "being courted as never before by the nation's retailers and manufacturers." The gauntlet would be thrown down. Turbulence would ensue. The landscape would no longer be featureless.

Visionary?

Yes, but the scheme to fix up the cellar into a rumpus room is a vision, too. The idealist deals with facts quite as much as the realist. He merely sees them differently, and it is that difference of viewpoint which we have had to live without for some years now. A more intimate relationship exists between the ideal and the "real" than it is currently fashionable to acknowledge. That relationship consists of the quintessential practicality of the ideal, and it was probably never better expressed than by Dr. A. J. Muste when he described utopianism as "the growing edge of society."

Indeed it is.

About the Author

MARGARET HALSEY's name as a writer was originally established with the publication of *With Malice Toward Some* (1938; republished in paperback 1959). During the Second World War, she worked for the Stage Door Canteen and other organizations; out of this experience came two more books—*Some of My Best Friends Are Soldiers* (1944) and *Color Blind* (1946). With her customary wit and perception, she further probed the American scene in *The Folks at Home* (1952) and *This Demi-Paradise* (1960). Miss Halsey was a lecturer on race relations at a time when the subject was far less openly discussed than today, and has been on the Board of Directors of the National Scholarship Service and Fund for Negro Students for fifteen years. She has also contributed to numerous magazines including the *New Republic*, the *Reporter*, and *Dissent*.

Margaret Halsey, who grew up in a New York suburb and was graduated from Skidmore College, now lives in White Plains, N.Y., with her husband and daughter.